D1575255

Epworth Commentaries

General Editors
Harold F. Guite and Ivor H. Jones

The Book of Job

Epworth Commentaries

Already published

The Gospel of John
Kenneth Grayston

The Book of Job
C.S. Rodd

In preparation

The Gospel of Matthew
Ivor Jones

The Gospel of Mark
Kenneth Howcroft

The Epistle to the Hebrews
Paul Ellingworth

The Johannine Epistles
William Loader

I and II Thessalonians
Neil Richardson

The Book of Psalms
Adrian Curtis

The Book of
JOB

C.S. RODD

EPWORTH PRESS

British Library Cataloguing in Publication Data

Rodd, Cyril S. (Cyril Stanley), *1928–*
The Book of Job.
1. Bible. O. T. Job – Critical studies
1. Title
223.106

ISBN 0–7162–0468–1

First published 1990
by Epworth Press
Room 195 1 Central Buildings, Westminster
London SW1H 9NR

Phototypeset by Input Typesetting Ltd, London
and printed in Great Britain by
Billing & Sons Ltd, Worcester

To the memory of my parents
My father who, like Job, suffered greatly
yet always retained the patience of the hero
of the folk story, and my mother who enabled him
to build his life anew.

CONTENTS

General Introduction   ix
Preface   xi
Acknowledgments   xii
Introduction   xiii
For Further Reading   xvii

I Job in his own times   1
   1–2   The story   1
   3   Job breaks the silence   10
   4–5   Eliphaz speaks first   13
   6–7   Job's response   18
   8   Bildad's first speech   21
   9–10   Job turns away from his friends   23
   11   Zophar speaks   27
   12–14   Job's response at the end of the first round
          of speeches   29
   15   Eliphaz describes the distress of the wicked 33
   16–17   Job's fluctuating moods   35
   18   Bildad sets out the fate of the wicked 37
   19   Job's plea for vindication   38
   20   Zophar describes what awaits the wicked 42
   21   Job flatly denies Zophar's argument   43
   22   Eliphaz asserts Job's guilt   45
   23–24   Job's answer to Eliphaz   47
   25   Bildad's final word   50
   26–27   A tangle of speeches   51
   28   God's unfathomable wisdom   53
   29–31   Job's final survey of his case   55
   32–33   The first speech of Elihu   63
   34   Elihu's second speech   66
   35   Elihu continues his argument   68
   36–37   The final speech of Elihu   69

38.1–40.5	God's first speech and Job's first submission	72
40.6–42.6	God's second speech; Job says he is satisfied	79
42.7–17	The epilogue	80

II The Author's Purpose 82

III Job: a Twentieth-century Christian Reading 91

1.	Job 1–2: Why Suffering?	92
2.	Job's curse and lament	95
3.	The failure of the friends	97
4.	Job speaks	102
5.	Where can wisdom be found?	113
6.	Job's life story and final plea	115
7.	Elihu	118
8.	Yahweh's speeches and Job's submissions	120
9.	The end of the story	125

Appendix 1: Ancient Parallels to Job	128
Appendix 2: Alternative Interpretations of Job	134
Appendix 3: The Problem of Evil	138

GENERAL INTRODUCTION

The *Epworth Preacher's Commentaries* that Greville P. Lewis edited so successfully in the 1950s and 1960s having now served their turn, the Epworth Press has commissioned a team of distinguished academics who are also preachers and teachers to create a new series of commentaries that will serve the 1990s and beyond. We have seized the opportunity offered by the publication in 1989 of the Revised English Bible to use this very readable and scholarly version as the basis of our commentaries, and we are grateful to the Oxford and Cambridge University Presses for the requisite license and for granting our authors pre-publication access. They will nevertheless be free to cite and discuss other translations wherever they think that these will illuminate the original text.

Just as the books that make up the Bible differ in their provenance and purpose, so our authors will necessarily differ in the structure and bearing of their commentaries. But they will all strive to get as close as possible to the intention of the original writers, expounding their texts in the light of the place, time, circumstance, and culture that gave them birth, and showing why each work was received by Jews and Christians into their respective Canons of Holy Scripture. They will seek to make full use of the dramatic advance in biblical scholarship world-wide but at the same time to explain technical terms in the language of the common reader, and to suggest ways in which Scripture can help towards the living of a Christian life today. They will endeavour to produce commentaries that can be used with confidence in ecumenical, multiracial, and multifaith situations, and not by scholars only but by preachers, teachers, students, church members, and anyone who wants to improve his or her understanding of the Bible.

Spring, 1990   Harold F. Guite

PREFACE

In this preface I simply want to thank all those who made this little book possible. John Stacey, who invited me to contribute to the series, and allowed me to select any book from the breadth of the Old Testament to write on. Ivor Jones, generous in praise, precise in detail. The writers of commentaries and articles, who have contributed so much to my thinking and who have mainly gone unacknowledged. Above all my wife, who has run the house, tended the garden, produced meals on time to the minute, and helped to keep *The Expository Times* going. Without her there would be no commentary at all.

ACKNOWLEDGEMENTS

I am grateful to the following publishers for permission to include quotations from copyright material:

A. & C. Black for *A Foreword to the Old Testament* by H. St. J. Hart, 1951

Methodist Publishing House for the Hymn by Donald Hughes (No. 6 in *Hymns and Songs*).

Orbis Books for *On Job* by Gustavo Gutiérrez, translated by Matthew J. O'Connell, 1987

Oxford University Press for *Babylonian Wisdom Literature* by W. G. Lambert, 1960

SCM Press for *Near Eastern Religious Texts Relating to the Old Testament*, ed. W. Beyerlin, 1978.

T. & T. Clark or *Canaanite Myths and Legends* by J. C. L. Gibson, 1978.

Princeton University Press for *Ancient Near Eastern Texts* ed. J. B. Pritchard, 1950 (cited as *ANET*).

INTRODUCTION

Everyone who tries to write a commentary on the book of Job faces a daunting task. The difficulties are immense.

1. It is one of the very greatest works of world literature. How can the commentator's stumbling phrases and cramped style make this masterpiece come alive to the reader? How can someone who has never suffered at all dare to attempt an explanation of a book which probes the sufferings of a tormented mortal so deeply and relentlessly? 'You will never play this until you have suffered', my piano teacher once said to one of my fellow students as he played a movement from a Mozart concerto, flawlessly, as I thought. The surface brilliance was there, but my teacher realized that the underlying sympathy and passion were missing. So it is with Job. To read with true understanding you have to have been tortured. This is why one of the most impressive commentaries comes from Latin America.

2. It has the most difficult text of any of the books of the Old Testament. Words which occur only once in the whole Hebrew Bible abound. What precisely do they mean? The central section of the book is in poetry. How can anyone whose mother tongue is not Hebrew catch the emotional overtones, even if the literal meaning of the words has been rightly discovered (and that is frequently uncertain)? How indeed can poetry ever cross over into another language, and a language that belongs to a different linguistic group at that?

3. It comes from a culture far removed from our own. The writer lived in an unpolluted world, where street lights did not blot out the stars and no television screens brought the world into his home and trivialized the whole of human drama. He lived in an uncluttered world where it was possible to think deeply and feel intensely and draw close to God. In the same way that we are unable ever to hear a Bach fugue as Bach's contemporaries heard it, for our ears have listened to Beethoven and Berlioz and Britten and the blues, so we can never recover the impression the book of Job made on those who

first heard it read aloud. Our attempts to determine its genre, trace the flow of its thought, seek out its background, understand its purpose, perhaps take it to pieces to discover how it was constructed and what its history was, are all futile. We can never know.

In a wonderfully evocative passage at the end of his introduction to the Old Testament, Henry St John Hart urges us to read the Old Testament itself before we turn to the commentaries, for to understand any work of literature or poetry we must read with attention, sympathy and imagination. Only by so reading shall we understand why the Old Testament became sacred wisdom in Jewry and why it forms part of the Christian Bible. Recalling what Dr Johnson had said elsewhere, he gives us this advice: Let the reader say softly, but resolutely, in his heart: 'Notes are often necessary but they are necessary evils. I am as yet unacquainted with the powers of these ancient writers. Every chapter that I read I will read from the first verse to the last with utter negligence of all the commentators. When my attention is strongly engaged let it disdain alike to turn aside to the name of Driver or Wellhausen. I will read on through brightness and obscurity, seeking only to preserve my comprehension of the broad line of the sermon, psalm, or story. I will let the modern European fabric of my daily vision fade far away, dissolve, be quite forgot. Until I understand my writer's ignorance I will presume myself ignorant of his understanding. Each verse is but a moment's monument, I will be reverent of its arduous fullness.'[1]

What then have been my methods and aim in writing this commentary?

I believe that there are few things more annoying to a congregation than to be told by the preacher that the text they can see plainly in front of them does not mean in the original Hebrew or Greek what they suppose it means. They assume, surely not without reason, that the translators were competent craftsmen and that at least a measure of the sense has been ferried across to an alien shore.

Although I have worked with the Hebrew Bible open in front of me, this little commentary is an exposition of the REB translation. Every translator is an interpreter. REB, like NEB before it, has adopted many rediscovered meanings of Hebrew words, and differences between it and the older versions of the Bible often spring from this. REB, like every translation, at times has had to emend an untranslatable text, not always noting the alterations in the margin. Sometimes I have found myself disagreeing with the decisions of the

[1] *A Foreword to the Old Testament*, A. & C. Black and OUP, New York, 1951, 177–8.

translators. Sometimes I have been puzzled as to how they arrived at their translation. But I have let it pass, believing that my task is to expound the meaning which the translators found in the text of Job. Where it brings flashes of insight I have directed the eyes of my readers to its beauties. Where I disagree with its phrasing I have mostly kept my peace. This is an English commentary for English readers of the English Bible.

I also believe that many people are alienated from scholarship because it seems to them that the main interest of scholars is to dissect, to dismantle, to take the biblical text to pieces. This is mistaken, but there is sufficient truth in it for me to follow another road: to accept the book as we have it in the Bible. It is a path that is being increasingly trodden today, and for that reason this commentary may well be regarded as either trendy or commonplace. But this is the only text we have. We may feel that it is inconsistent in places, that sections have been added at some later stage in its development, that isolated verses have been misplaced (and indeed REB naughtily transposes verses on occasion), but if we follow St John Hart's sound wisdom we shall read what stands before us, attempting to discern what it meant to the final editor, even if this was not what the first poet wrote. This does not mean that I attach any particular authority to the present text. I think that such claims are misplaced and that a relaxed attitude to scripture allows it to speak its message more effectively. Words like 'revelation' and 'inspiration' set us on a false trail. Only by surrendering our domination over the text and refusing to determine beforehand what we will allow it to say shall we begin to grasp its truth. It behoves the Christian to be humble.

There still remains a major difficulty for the commentator, perhaps the greatest difficulty of all. Inevitably a commentary moves step by step, picking up a verse or a group of verses, stopping, going back to the beginning, making observations, halting the flow until the explanation has been uttered, and then starting off afresh. Thus the commentator erects a series of barrages across the stream, damming up the waters to an unnatural depth, flooding the banks and destroying the sparkle of the living river. This is disastrous for a book like Job, where the reader must read on through chapter after chapter until he reaches the end. Not only so, but the book only discloses its teaching to the one who has read the whole. The temptation, therefore, is simply to write an extended introduction to the book, for how is a commentary possible?

One fact alone emboldens the commentator to attempt his task. The poem was originally spoken. And spoken words are heard one after another in a line. The hearer has to remember what came before. (Why are students so hostile to memorising information? Unless we remember the beginning of a sentence we cannot make sense of the end. If we cannot relate what we learnt on several different occasions, we are unable to progress in wisdom.) I shall try to avoid splitting the book into fragments that are too small to contribute to the meaning of the whole. The speech will be the unit. But a well constructed paragraph possesses a structure, and within the speeches I shall attempt to show the way the thought develops and is expressed, and this will involve turning to smaller sections of text.

There is one further word that must be said. This is a Christian commentary. Our interest in the book of Job is different from our interest in the epic of Gilgamesh or the Bhagavad-gita. Perhaps it should not be so. Perhaps all religious texts offer to us equal opportunities to ponder the mysteries of the universe and to travel into the country of the spirit. But I suspect that few of those who read these words would have thought it worthwhile to buy this book had they not found Job within the Christian scriptures. Moreover, none of us can escape our background and presuppositions. We see what our eyes have been taught to see by the culture in which we were nurtured. I write, therefore, as a stumbling Christian, too long immured among shelves of books even to have properly lived out the Christian way. A little symbol of this is my preference for BC and AD to the more modish BCE and CE. It will serve to remind the reader that however much we try to enter into the world of the writer of Job, that world will ever remain strange to us. We are aliens and pilgrims, constantly translating what we observe into ideas and patterns of thought which have meaning for our situation.

Because I believe it is important to try to think ourselves back into the world of the thoughts and emotions of the poet who created this majestic work, I have moved to this Christian interpretation in two stages. First I shall guide the reader through the book, seeking to recover something of the poet's own meaning. It will require the stripping off of many twentieth-century ideas. Then, having gained some appreciation of what the poet was saying, we shall look at the book as a whole, considering the intention of the poet and the questions which his work raises. Finally we shall travel along the road a second time, now asking what the poet's words have to say to a Christian reader today.

With this much introduction, let us begin.

FOR FURTHER READING

Two major modern commentaries are based on the Hebrew text, but the exegesis and discussions of the message of the book are accessible to those without any knowledge of the language:

Norman C. Habel, *The Book of Job*, SCM Press and Westminster Press 1985

John E. Hartley, *The Book of Job*, Eerdmans 1988

Of medium length and intended for teaching and preaching, though in rather a heavy style, is:

J. Gerald Janzen, *Job*, John Knox Press 1985

Among the smaller commentaries I would single out:

John C. L. Gibson, *Job*, Saint Andrew Press 1985

If it can be found in libraries or second-hand, an older commentary has much still to offer after three-quarters of a century:

James Strahan, *The Book of Job Interpreted*, T. & T. Clark and Scribner's 1913

Among the general discussions of the book the following may be commended:

J. H. Eaton, *Job* (Old Testament Guides), JSOT Press 1985

R. Gordis, *The Book of God and Man*, University of Chicago Press 1965 (by an American Jewish scholar)

Sermon topics and outlines which are sure to excite the interest of preacher and congregation are provided in:

Norman C. Habel, *Job* (Knox Preaching Guides), John Knox Press 1981

A book which everyone should read, coming as it does from a Liberation theologian in Latin America is:

Gustavo Gutiérrez, *On Job: God-talk and the Suffering of the Innocent*, Orbis 1987

Finally two articles which appeared in the *Bulletin of the John Rylands Library* provide general surveys of scholarship up to 1971:

H. H, Rowley, 'The Book of Job and its Meaning', vol. 41, 1958–59, pp. 167–207, reprinted in *From Moses to Qumran*, Lutterworth Press and Association Press 1963, pp. 141–83

James Barr, 'The Book of Job and its Modern Interpreters', vol. 54, 1971–72, pp. 28–46

David J. A. Clines, *Job 1–20*, *Job 21–42* (Word Biblical Commentary, vols. 17 and 18), Word Books 1989–90, was published too late to be used in this commentary. It is the most exciting commentary on Job that I have read and offers many fascinating insights into the meaning of the book.

I

Job in his own Times

1–2   *The story*

The outline of the book of Job is easy to follow. It begins and ends with the story, told in simple prose. Within this framework the poet has set a dialogue between Job and his three friends, Eliphaz, Bildad and Zophar. Job speaks first and then speeches by each of the friends alternate with further speeches by Job. The debate continues like this three times, although at the end the arguments of the friends falter and Job is left to address God alone. Finally a fourth speaker comes forward, a younger man, who is dismayed that the friends have been unable to produce convincing arguments against Job. So Elihu makes a long speech, or series of speeches, for six chapters. At last God calls to Job out of the whirlwind, and Job submits to him.

All the greatest poets have taken the most simple, almost humdrum things and lifted them to pure magic. Browning took the rather sordid story of a murder trial in the 'Yellow Book' which he found on a bookstall in Rome and produced what is perhaps his finest achievement, *The Ring and the Book*, probing the deep questions of character and motive, prejudice and justice. So here the poet of so long ago took a folk story, retold it, and then poured into it verse which continues to offer fresh insights into the meaning of suffering and goodness, doubt and faith.

The first and perhaps most important thing to notice about the story of Job is that it is not an account of a Christian or even a Jew. The name is not a Hebrew name, and the writer of the book seems deliberately to have avoided placing either his hero or the friends in Israel.

Where Uz was is unknown. Tradition looks to two quite separate locations, to the south of Judah in the region of Edom, and in the north of Palestine in the area of Syria. For our purposes it is sufficient to notice that it is outside of Israel.

The name Job was known to Ezekiel (Ezek. 14.14, 20), but he does no more than list him with the two other great and good men from ancient times, Noah and Daniel (not the Daniel of the book of Daniel, but a much older hero who is now known to us from the texts which were discovered in Ugarit, the modern Ras Shamra, coming from the fourteenth century BC). It is pointless to try to determine the meaning of the name. Our poet has taken an ancient hero, and a traditional folk story.

The three friends also do not come from Israel. Genealogies in the Old Testament record an Eliphaz who was eldest son of Esau and the father of Teman (Gen. 36.11, 15), but our poet hardly intended the same person. Teman is one of the chief places in Edom, a country renowned for its wise men (Jer. 49.7; Obad. 8–9). Bildad does not occur elsewhere in the Hebrew Bible, but his name too has been linked with names from Assyria and elsewhere. Shuah is mentioned in Gen. 25.2, and is known outside of the Old Testament as a country on the middle Euphrates. The name Zophar also is restricted to the book of Job, and although there was a Naamah in Judah (Josh. 15.41), our poet almost certainly intended a place outside of Palestine, but again its precise location is unknown.

The exact identification of the people and their homes is of slight importance. But they direct our attention to two very important features of the book.

1. Our poet, whoever he was (and this also matters little for an understanding of the religious message) was a Jew whose mother tongue was Hebrew. Yet he had the widest of intellectual and religious interests and could roam freely among the wisdom literature of the ancient world. In the prose story he uses the personal name of Israel's God freely. (The name is found in the Hebrew Bible only with the consonants YHWH, but it is highly probable that it was pronounced Yahweh, with short vowels and the accent on the second syllable. REB follows the tradition that is found as early as the old Greek translation of the Pentateuch. This boldly followed Jewish precedent and replaced Yahweh with the LORD.) In the poem Job and the friends never refer to God by name, apart from 12.9.[1] The high issues of God and humanity, creation and suffering, justice and reward, are matters for the whole world and cannot be confined to people of a single religious tradition.

The countries surrounding Israel had much to contribute. There was the story of a righteous nobleman in Babylon who suffered greatly and was finally restored by his god Marduk. There were

---

[1] Though many scholars emend the text here.

attempts to come to terms with the problem of suffering. Psalmists in Israel and in Egypt lamented the plight of human beings in a world where reward and punishment do not seem to be rightly meted out to good and evil men and women. Scholars debate whether our poet drew upon these writings as he composed his work. It hardly seems possible to conceive that he was not aware of them. So for a full understanding of the poem we need to read an ancient Sumerian document, often called 'Sumerian Job', 'I will praise the Lord of wisdom' (the so-called 'Babylonian Job'), and the dialogue between a sufferer and his friend which has been named the 'Babylonian Theodicy'.

The problem of suffering was felt in Babylon, as it was for many in Israel, because for both of these peoples death was the end. There was no future life, and so any recompense had to be worked out in this life. It was particularly acute in Israel because monotheism meant that Yahweh was directly responsible for suffering. In Mesopotamia there were many gods and many demons, and this might ease the problem, yet even there it was felt that the gods should protect their devotees from harm.

In Egypt there was a lively hope of life after death and the problem of suffering seems not to have arisen with the same intensity. Nevertheless there are writings which may be compared with Job: 'The Protests of the Eloquent Peasant' and the 'Dispute over Suicide'.[2]

Some have found similarities to Job in the story of Keret from Ugarit. Keret was a king who is described as 'noble' or 'generous'. He suffered the loss of his children and later became ill. Somewhat like Job he was accused (by his son) of failing to judge the cause of the widow and the poor and not feeding the orphan. The story differs markedly from Job, however, in that Keret's chief concern is to secure a new family rather than with the problem of suffering and a man's relation with his God.

Looking more widely still, there are various prayers, complaints, and petitions in both the biblical book of Psalms and in the literatures of other peoples in the ancient Middle East which probably influenced our poet as he composed Job's speeches, in many of which Job turns away from his friends to pray directly to God. Some scholars suggest that we shall learn more about the meaning of the book by looking at these prayers than by limiting our gaze to discussions of the problem of suffering.

2. Our poet writes for fellow Jews. But his message reaches out to

---

[2] Outlines and extracts will be found in Appendix I.

the whole world. His book has become part of the Christian Bible as well as of the Jewish scriptures. His theme is one which is as universal as the suffering of which he speaks, and in this century we cannot overlook the place which it has in the great world faiths, and in particular in the religions of India. By choosing men who were not Jews as his actors, yet by taking us into the heavenly court of Yahweh and by introducing Yahweh at the end of his poem, he reminds us that in the end he can only speak of the problem of suffering as he sees it as a worshipper of the Jewish God.

This means that we shall understand the book only as we attempt to place ourselves where he is. What was the religious background to his work?

There are three streams of thought about reward and punishment in ancient Israel.

(*a*) The books from Deuteronomy to II Kings are generally regarded as the work of a single school of writers. Throughout the history there is the underlying belief that obedience will secure Israel's prosperity, but that when Israel sins God punishes by sending foreign enemies to defeat her armies. The scheme is worked out vividly in the book of Judges. Later the destruction of Northern Israel by Assyria and the capture of Jerusalem by the Babylonians are said to be due to the people's sin.

(*b*) The prophets foretold national disaster as punishment of social evils. Similar to the Deuteronomists' philosophy of history, they look to war, earthquake, plague, locusts and drought as God's way of dealing with his sinful people, and like the Deuteronomists they link reward and punisment with obedience and wrongdoing. Later the books of Jeremiah and Ezekiel extend this belief (Jer. 31.29–30; Ezek. 18). It is not only the nation which will be punished by God; the individual Israelite will receive the due reward for his actions.

(*c*) The writers of proverbs and the composers of some of the Psalms were equally convinced that act and recompense exactly correspond. It is almost automatic (e.g. Prov. 10.2; 11.6–8; 13.18; 19.16; 22.4; Pss. 1; 37.1–4, 25, 27–29, 37–38), and generally there is little questioning. Sometimes the writers felt a twinge of hesitation, and responded to it by suggesting that the retribution would be meted out to the evil man's children, or that although the wicked appeared to prosper at the moment, soon disaster would strike (Prov. 13.22, cf. Ps. 37.10–13, 35–36). Real doubts appear only in Pss. 49 and 73.

Reward and retribution were so firmly entrenched in the thought of ancient Israel that some writers rewrite history so that it conforms to their theology. The Chronicler invents a repentance for Manasseh to account for his long reign (II Chron. 33.10–20, cf. II Kings 21.1–18) and makes Josiah disobey Necho's words 'spoken at God's command' to explain his early death (II Chron. 35.21–22, cf. II Kings 23.29).[3]

There has been intense debate about the relation between the story and the poetic dialogue. Some have pointed to the marked contrasts between them: the use of the name Yahweh in the story and its absence in the poem; the different characterization of Job – patient and passive in the story, defiant and questioning in the dialogue; the scene in heaven which plays no part at all in the poetic sections of the book; perhaps a difference in the situation of Job: in the story depicted as a powerful rural sheik, in the poem much more a town-dweller. Surely the two parts of the book did not originally belong together. Those who do not wish to tear the two sections from each other by arguing that a later editor linked them together, suggest that perhaps the poet did not venture to alter the folk-tale which he adopted as a setting for his poem, untroubled by the tensions that this set up. Others attempt to reduce the contrasts: it would be natural that the friends and Job would not use Israel's name for God since they are not Jews; even if Job may appear rebellious in the poem he never 'curses' God as his wife urged him to do; the test would fail if Job and the friends knew of the wager in heaven; and Job is seen to be a wealthy landowner in both story and poem. In the end no more than speculation is possible. We had better try to interpret the text as it stands.

Our poet is a master of prose as well as of poetry. Consider how deftly he has told his story. It begins like one of the parables of Jesus or the story that Nathan presented to King David. *There lived in the land of Uz a man of blameless and upright life named Job.* No links with any previous history. No filling in of an elaborate background. He simply begins his story.

One of the most striking features of many of the novels of Conrad is the way the action is limited to a very small number of individuals. The vivid descriptions of the scenery make it come alive, but those who walk in that world are few. And almost always underlying the action is some serious moral issue. There is Falk, who had once kept himself alive by resorting to cannibalism. His drawing of his hands down his face is symbolic of the anguish from which he can never escape. In *The End of the Tether* we sail with Captain Whalley, going blind and so unable to steer his ship properly, yet anxious to complete

---

[3] On this wider question see R. Davidson, *The Courage to Doubt*, SCM Press 1983.

his term of service for the sake of his daughter, to whom he will give the money he is earning and carefully saving. By narrowing the focus down to one individual Conrad enables us to feel the full impact of these ethical dilemmas and the psychological stresses under which his heroes are placed.

So with Job. It is as if the writer is saying, 'If you want to understand what suffering means look at Job.' And in the book Job is more than the hero, more than the main speaker in the dialogue. He is the archetypal sufferer, and through his anguished speaking we both come to feel the problem of suffering and watch the way faith and religious experiences can be deepened through that suffering.

1.1–5   The picture of Job is extravagant. He is of blameless and upright life, holding God in reverence and opposed to all wrong doing. His sons are seven, the sacred number, and in that patriarchal age his blessing is complete for he has more sons than daughters. Sheep, camels, oxen, and the highly prized she-donkeys form his massive estate. He has a large number of servants (or slaves, though this word must not make us think of the cotton plantations of the USA; in any case he is a good master who looks after his slaves well, see 31.13–15).

The idyllic scene is completed with the apparently endless round of feasting by his sons, and Job's goodness is secured by the glimpse at his anxious sacrifices for his children, just in case they might have sinned when the wine had flowed too freely.

Too good to be true? In some ways perhaps it is. And yet we shall completely misread the whole rest of the book unless we take this description of Job seriously. When Job sets before God the record of his moral life (ch. 31) it matches this portrait that our poet has sketched out in the first five verses of his book. This is intended to be an accurate account of the man who will later suffer so grievously.

1.6–12   The scene abruptly changes to heaven. In ancient Israel Yahweh was pictured as a King within his heavenly court. There are parallels in the ideas of the 'assembly of the gods' in the literature of the ancient Middle East, and in the Old Testament Yahweh sits among the heavenly beings in Pss. 29.1; 82; 89.5–8; I Kings 22.19–23. To call them angels is to invoke the wrong overtones today. They are Yahweh's servants and courtiers. Among them is *the Adversary, Satan*. As we can see from the continuation of the story (1.7, 9, 12) and in the second heavenly assembly in 2.1–6, although Satan later became a proper name,[4] here it represents rather the office which 'the Satan' holds – grand inquisitor, public prosecutor, though with a suggestion that he believes the worst of everyone and always searches for hidden motives and evil desires. In Job, indeed, he is 'the Adversary', stirring up trouble, a spy, who ranges over the earth from end to end.

If we had any doubt about the validity of the poet's description of Job's goodness at the beginning of the story, such doubt is immediately quelled. God uses exactly the same phrase of his servant. One of the features of the story is the use of repetition, which adds to its charm in the way that stories told to children come back over and over again to the same key set of words, and also adds emphasis to ideas that are important for our poet. The phrase will reappear in 2.3. Right at the start and after the first test has been successfully completed God vouches for Job's integrity.

Then the Adversary's cynicism bursts out. Job has good reason to be good. He has been rewarded for his goodness. (Note the phrase: *have you not hedged him round on every side with your protection. . ?* It will find a cruel echo later when Job speaks.) But what if Job loses his family and his possessions?

In his study of what he terms 'The Cross in Job', Wheeler Robinson draws attention to the way we frequently speak of trusting in God, and indeed it is an important part of religious faith. But, he suggests, 'is there not often a neglected truth in the thought that God is trusting us?'[5] In 1.12 we see that trust. The Adversary had challenged God. Strip off all that Job possesses, kill his family, *then* his piety will be turned into cursing.

As suddenly as it moved to heaven, the scene returns to earth (1.13–22). To add poignancy, and to make the destruction of all Job's children on the same day possible, the sons and daughters are feasting in their eldest brother's house – is there perhaps a hidden suggestion that this was the grandest of the seven feasts when they went the rounds? In this section of the story the poet's use of repetition comes to the fore: the arrival of the messengers one after another, the almost identical words, the conclusion of each message, *only I have escaped to bring you the news,* leading to the final blow, the young people are dead. The means of the destruction are varied – this is no hack poet – but the differences are for dramatic and literary effect rather than because destruction is by a particular disaster, and there is no need to concern ourselves with the Sabaeans, the

---

[4] I Chron. 21.1 and in post-biblical Jewish writings, and the New Testament.
[5] *The Cross in the Old Testament*, SCM Press 1955, Westminster Press 1956, 47.

Chaldaeans, the lightning, or the whirlwind. Man-made and natural disasters alternate – though it is only we who call the lightning and whirlwind 'natural'.

Job's response is to turn to mourning and to God. Pedantic, literally minded scholars ask how Job could return to the womb, and REB has flinched from the AV's 'thither'. This is poetry. Naked at birth, naked in death, life and death are in Yahweh's hands; praise be to him.

The Adversary's challenge has failed, and our poet points it out.

But should Job have accepted his loss in this way? No one who has read Camus's *The Plague* can avoid the question. Hold it in your mind as we turn to the second chapter.

2.1–6   So back to the scene in heaven and Yahweh's court. Again the poet uses repetition to recall the first confrontation between Yahweh and the Adversary. But Yahweh goes further now. In words that partly reflect a sense of triumph that he has won his wager and partly reveal his sense of guilt, Yahweh points out that Job *still holds fast to his integrity*, even though the Satan had incited God *to ruin him without cause*. But the Satan is unbowed. Everyone is self-centred, he says. Loss of possessions, even loss of children can be borne. But what if illness strikes the man himself? The stakes are now raised, and again Yahweh takes up the challenge. And again he leaves the Adversary to carry out his dirty work. *Just reach out your hand and touch his bones and his flesh*, the Satan had said. Yahweh's response is, *He is in your power; only spare his life.*[6]

2.7.10   So Job is struck down with disease. It is pointless to attempt to determine what illness was intended. Here it is clearly a skin disease. In the dialogue Job describes his illness in more detail (7.4–5, 13–15; 16.16; 19.17, 20; 30.17, 27, 30), but again we should be wrong to attempt any clinical diagnosis. To understand the meaning of the poet it is sufficient to see in the disease an affliction which Job's contemporaries will interpret as direct punishment by God for some

[6] There is a double play on words in the Hebrew which cannot be reproduced in English. First, the word translated 'power' is literally 'hand': the Adversary had told God to stretch out *his* hand and strike Job with illness; God places Job in the Adversary's 'hand', thus reinforcing the fact that God is willing to allow Job to be 'punished' for wrongs that he has not committed, but keeps his own hands clean. Second, the Hebrew word for 'spare' is literally 'keep'. The word is used in 29.2 and Ps. 16.1 of God's protecting care. In 10.14; 13.27 Job will accuse God of 'watching, spying on' him. Habel finds deep irony here: 'Without knowing, Job accuses God of playing the spying role of the Satan, while the Satan is expected to play the role of God by protecting Job' (*The Book of Job*, 1985, p. 95).

sin that he has committed. Here lies his real anguish. The physical pain is great, but worse is the meaning which the disease carries. The reference to sitting among the *ashes*, the refuse heaps outside of the town, is a further indication that Job is now cut off not only from human society but also from the religious community. As a 'sinner' he is an outcast.

Women are pushed to the edges of a patriarchal society. Our story-teller makes no mention of the suffering which the death of her sons and daughters has caused Job's wife. She is simply cast as a further temptation to Job. *Curse God and die!* is a call to take the only sure way out of his evil plight. If God is cursed openly, he will finally kill Job and his sufferings will be ended. Job, however, retains his pious attitude towards God. He accepts that everything comes from God. There is no escape from this grim fact, either by positing hostile gods or by supposing that the sufferings are part of the natural order. To understand the meaning of the book we need to return to a world in which every event in nature is directly caused by God (see Ps. 104 for a poetic expression of this belief).

2.11–13   Verse 11 introduces the three friends and makes the connection between the prose story and the poetic dialogue. 'Job's comforters' has become a byword in ordinary speech for those who come in the guise of friends but actually aggravate someone's distress. And indeed this is what happens in the end. But that was not their intention. We need to notice that they were real friends. They came long distances to show their sympathy and to bring comfort. They made elaborate arrangements for the journey. And so great was their grief when they first set eyes on him that they fell into extravagant mourning, and then came to where he was, on the refuse heap outside the town, and *sat beside him*.

What went wrong? To discover the full answer to this question we need to read the whole of the dialogue. For the moment we do well to fasten on the true sympathy which they show, in silence sharing his suffering, sitting with him, outcasts alongside the outcast. It is the best of men who increase Job's pain. It is the best of intentions which lead to harsh words and unkind judgments.

This is the part of Job which most people know best, indeed which may be all they know. The story is heart-rending and told with supreme skill, using repetition and word play to such good effect. As a folk-story it might have been intended to sustain a piety of submission to the griefs and pains that afflict all human life. This is what is emphasized: *Throughout all this, Job did not utter one sinful word,* says the poet. Twice Yahweh has triumphantly pointed to *my servant Job*, adding, *You will find no one like him on earth, a man of blameless and upright life, who fears God and sets his face against wrongdoing.* The argument of the whole depends upon the truth of Job's goodness and integrity.

Who is on trial in the book? Job's piety is certainly being tested to the limits of human endurance. In a sense the theology of the friends is being tested in the fires of events. And since Job holds the same theology as the friends, his theology is being tested in the fire of experience. But what of God? Is there no truth also on the side of those scholars who question the goodness and integrity of God? What kind of a God is it who will so easily take up the Satan's challenge? What kind of a God is it who can say, *You incited me to ruin him without cause*, and then allow himself to be persuaded to afflict Job still more?

3   Job breaks the silence

The seven days of silence are ended by this outburst by Job. It is not addressed to the friends. It is barely addressed to God, although only God is capable of providing any answers to Job's urgent questions. It is a bitter cry for death since death alone seems to offer any hope of comfort and rest.

The structure of the chapter is not entirely clear. Some find a curse (vv. 1–13 or 1–10) followed by a lament (vv. 14–26 or 11–26). REB treats it as a single complaint in four parts, which might perhaps be entitled: Job's curse on the day of his conception and the day of his birth (vv. 1–10), Job's wish that he had died at birth (vv. 11–15), Job's questions about suffering in the light of the quiet ease of the abode of the dead (vv. 17–23), and Job's description of his present anguish (vv. 24–26).[1]

There are certain parallels with Gen. 1, which have led some to interpret the chapter as a call to reverse the creation and return to primeval chaos, the rest on the seventh day being transformed in vv.

---

[1] REB has omitted v. 2, presumably because it sounded repetitious in English, and transferred v. 16 to follow v. 12. Certainly to our Western sense of style and logic both are to be preferred, but there is no textual evidence for moving the verse and we cannot be sure what was the intention of the poet or how the chapter would have struck the original hearers.

11–26 from the joyous rest of the Sabbath to the silent rest of Sheol.[2] Our poet can be savage. Darkness is to replace light. Leviathan was the monster with whom Baal battled in the stories from Ugarit, and is Yahweh's opponent in Ps. 74.14 and Isa. 27.1.[3] Those whose spells are strong enough to bind the powers of destruction will assuredly be able to destroy the day of Job's birth.

There are some resemblances to the 'Dispute over Suicide', in which the Egyptian poet describes death in terms of ease and pleasure, such as the recovery of a sick man, release from prison, enjoying sweet scents, and sitting in the shade on a breezy day. It is impossible to say whether our poet knew this writing or not. Jer. 20.14–18 is so similar that one of the writers must have known the other, unless both were drawing on a common tradition.

3.1–10   The idea of cursing the day of one's birth is strange to us. It may be that underlying the practice is a belief that each day continued to exist and came round again each year. The meaning of the curse would then be that Job's birthday itself should cease to exist because of the suffering which he has had to endure. Presumably his own destruction would follow. On the other hand this may be a poetic way of expressing a wish that the sufferer had never been born, indeed, had never even been conceived.

3.11–15   The wish to have died at birth is a little more intelligible than some other parts of Job. It has to be remembered, however, that for most of the Old Testament there was no hope of a happy future life. Ideas of resurrection and eternal life came extremely late into Israelite religion, the only absolutely certain reference being Dan. 12.1–2, in a book which can be dated fairly precisely as between 167 and 164 BC, although there may be glimpses in Isa. 26.19 and Pss. 16.9–10; 49.15; 73.24. The general picture of what happens after death was gloomy. Several of the Psalms provide a picture of Sheol, a kind

---

[2] v. 4a ('day', 'darkness'): Gen. 1.5 and 3 ('day', 'light').

v. 4b ('God above'): Gen. 1.7 ('waters above')

v. 5a ('darkness'): Gen. 1.2, 4 ('darkness')

v. 6 ('night', 'days of the year'): Gen. 1.14 ('night', 'days', 'years')

v. 8 ('Leviathan'): Gen. 1.21 ('sea monsters'). REB's 'sea monster' is based on an emendation.

v. 9 ('light'): Gen. 1.15 ('light')

The theme of the reversal of creation and the return of chaos is also found in Jer. 4.23–26.

[3] Leviathan is also found in Ps. 104.26, but there appears to be some natural animal. REB suggests Leviathan is the whale in 41.1, and it is a little surprising that the same identification was not made here.

of communal grave, into which the dead go. Even the greatest king becomes weak as he descends into this land of shades and dust and forgetfulness, where no one can any longer praise God. Those who abide there are outside the reach of God's thought and beyond his care.[4] This is the belief which underlies the book of Job. Our poet is unwilling to grasp at a happy future life as a recompense for the sufferings of the present. At this point the emphasis is upon release from suffering, whether as captives or slaves or weary labourers, freed from the attacks of the wicked and the commands of the slave-driver.

Job's wish, therefore, is very close to a longing for total extinction. In Sheol he would have the peace of sleep, and had he died at birth none of his present sufferings would have come upon him.

3.17–23   One feature of the book of Job is the way in which Job's sufferings are broadened out to include all men (the masculine is appropriate, for there are few references to women in the poem, although as we shall see there is a special place for Job's daughters right at the end). In vv. 17–23 Job includes all sufferers within his longing for ease.

We have already noticed that the writer of Job was a master of words and irony. A telling little example is found in v. 23. The Satan had complained that God had always protected Job, he had *hedged him round on every side with* [his] *protection* (1.10). Here Job uses the same word (spelled slightly differently), but with very different overtones. The weary suffering is *hedged about by God on every side*. Instead of being a protector, God has now become the jailor, the one who shuts men in and imposes limitations upon their freedom. We must be alert for Job's perception of God in the later chapters.

Has Job turned at last? Is this the curse which his wife had urged upon him and which he had roundly rejected in 2.10? Some have thought it is – and have gone on to contrast the pious, submissive Job of the story with the rebel of the poem. Could the same author have combined both in a single work? The answer must be that we do not know. But the dialogue cannot be understood without some background, and the prologue is as good as any. The goodness of Job had to be affirmed. The friends had to be introduced. The proceedings of the heavenly council remain unknown to Job and the friends, but they may well have been necessary for the author's purpose. And is the contrast between the two Jobs so impossible? It

[4] See Pss. 6.5; 30.8; 88.10–12; 115.17; cf. Isa. 14.9–11.

may be that Job at last snapped. In the seven days of silence he had been brooding upon his sufferings and his good deeds. Now he can remain silent no longer.

At this point, however, the sufferings are uppermost in his mind. The question of God's justice has not yet come into his thought. As in the complaints in many of the psalms, the dominant request is for release rather than justice. But Job's outspoken comments disturb the friends. Eliphaz speaks first.

4–5   Eliphaz speaks first

There have been many attempts to discern differences in character between the three friends, but it is uncertain how far this can be done, or indeed how far it was intended by our poet. Certainly ancient Israel knew how to depict individuals – we have only to think of the vivid presentations of some of the women who appear in the pages of the Old Testament: the capable and energetic Rebekah ever ready to take firm decisions (Gen. 24, 27), both Tamars, deeply wronged, one resourceful, the other eloquent even in her distress (Gen. 38, II Sam. 13), the beautiful and perhaps artful Bathsheba (II Sam. 11, I Kings 1), and many more. To some extent, however, the friends all present the same traditional theology in somewhat similar ways, and it may be that dramatic effect was alien to the wisdom writers. We must avoid trying to turn this ancient writing into a modern play or introducing analyses which are more appropriate to the English novel. On the other hand, there are differences in the friends' attitudes to Job and in the way they present their case, and it may be worth pausing to consider these as we meet each friend for the first time.

Elihu sees the three as men much older than himself (32.4, 6), and since great reverence was accorded to age it is likely that Eliphaz should be pictured as the eldest of them all. His first speech reveals a kindly man, eager to offer sympathy and to give help to Job in his distress. He is also something of a mystic and tells of a vision which came to him in the middle of the night (4.12–21). He relies on experience as well as traditional lore, and is perhaps the one possessing the deepest religious feelings. Yet even he will fail Job in the end, and will end up by listing the sins which he suggsts Job must have committed.

It is not easy to decide how the speeches should be divided up. Some recent scholars think they can discern elaborate patterns of ideas and words. Apart from doubting whether our poet intended such artificial schemes or even used them unconsciously, they require a knowledge of the Hebrew text for a proper understanding and are too remote from preaching and teaching for the purposes of this commentary. Rather we shall follow the more obvious surface meanings, heedless of the accusations of superficiality which this will arouse.

4.2 Eliphaz appears shocked by the tone of Job's outburst – twice he refers to Job's lack of 'patience' (vv. 2, 5). He begins tentatively. Will anything anyone tries to say ease Job's pain? Will it not rather increase his anguish and rebellion? Yet who can remain silent?

4.3–5 How different Job is now from the man he was before the disaster struck! Then he was the strong one, who gave ready encouragement to those in distress. Now all that confident assurance has vanished.

4.6–11 Surely traditional wisdom should reassure him. And Eliphaz trots out the stock beliefs. No innocent person has ever perished. It is the confidence of the Psalmist (Ps. 37.3–4, 18–19, 23–26) – we can almost hear Eliphaz reciting this psalm, for he goes on to affirm the destruction which comes remorselessly upon those who do evil, exactly as the Psalmist does (Ps. 37.1–2, 9–10, 12–17, 20, 35–36, 38), and like the Psalmist he bases his faith upon his own experience of life. Eliphaz picks up several of the words which described Job in the Prologue: 'piety', 'blameless life', 'upright', although, of course, he is as unaware of the scene in Yahweh's heavenly court as Job is. It serves to reiterate Job's blamelessness, and at this point there is no hint that Eliphaz does not mean what he says. It is not only that Job is confident of his integrity; those who know him are equally ready to acknowledge his goodness. The exact purpose of vv. 10–11 is not entirely clear. REB has problems with the translation, for the poet has used five different words for 'lion'! Presumably the lion is a metaphor for the wicked. In the Babylonian Theodicy the friend also introduces a lion: 'Come, consider the lion that you mentioned, the enemy of cattle. For the crime which the lion committed the pit awaits him.'

4.12–16 Eliphaz now describes his vision. The atmosphere is

'creepy'. The sense of the uncanny is all-pervasive. At the moment in the night when the deepest sleep overcomes us all he is roused by an apparition. It is beside the point to inquire whether the mysterious visitant is an 'angel', and if we use the word we must avoid any ideas of figures with wings, clothed in white: that would be far from the world of ideas in which the poet lived. Equally we cannot be sure whether the poet intended the experience to be part of a nightmare or whether Eliphaz had roused from his sleep. The *deepest sleep* reminds us of Adam (Gen. 2.21) and Abraham (Gen. 15.12): the silence out of which the low whisper comes (*I heard a voice murmur*) recalls the experience of Elijah (I Kings 19.12). The essential point is that what Eliphaz meets is a messenger from God with a revelation for him. And that is strange. The wise men often relied upon traditional teaching passed down from generation to generation, from scribe to scribe, backed up by their own observation of how the world was ordered. We shall see this in the words of some of the other friends very plainly.

The message when it comes is disappointing. Everyone knows that no one can be righteous. Yet there is a little more than this. Our poet has linked the fragility of human life with the sinfulness of men and women and their failure to find wisdom. We shall have to consider what wisdom means later on. For the moment it is sufficient to regard it as a right moral understanding. Job sees in the contrast between God's great power and his own weakness a sign of God's cruelty and one reason why he will never be able to obtain justice. That is not Eliphaz's point. He accepts that everyone is weak and sinful, so that no one can claim that he deserves a lifetime of happiness. It is a valid point. Not everything which the friends say is false, and there is no reason to suppose that our poet intended us to assume it is. To acknowledge this, however, is not to go along with those who hold that the poet's answer to the problem of suffering is to be found in the arguments of the friends.

5.1   The first verse of ch. 5 is difficult. Probably it should be seen as a reinforcement of the theme of universal frailty and sinfulness, set against a belief that only those who are holy can expect to be heard by God or the members of his heavenly court.

5.2–7   Eliphaz then continues much like the psalmist – an indication that he is repeating stock ideas. He claims that he has observed punishment falling upon wicked men and upon their children (*fools* has moral overtones just as wisdom had). The idea of punishment being unleashed upon a man's children if he happens to escape it himself is completely alien to us. We may be a little uneasy about punishment in the sense of retribution, in any case, but to inflict injury upon the children seems blatantly unjust. It offends against our moral sense. A large part of the reason for this is that we have a highly individualistic view of humanity. Rather like Ezekiel (ch. 18), we hold that each person is responsible for what he or she has done. As the blame cannot be passed to someone else, neither can the punishment. The ancient Israelites thought in different ways. They hardly had a different kind of mentality. Some scholars even deny that they applied responsibility to the group rather than to the individual. It seems incontestable, however, that the idea that there was a kind of inherited guilt and therefore the children might suffer for the wrongdoing of their father was common in Old Testament times and within several different groups in Israel (see Exod. 20.5; Isa. 65.6–7; Jer. 31.27–30; 32.18; Pss. 79.8; 109.14). Evil deeds and suffering are linked inextricably. Since no one is sinless, no one escapes ill fortune.

5.8–16   After this general moralizing Eliphaz returns to address Job's situation afresh. 'If I were in your shoes' is his approach – and Job will round on this in due course. Since Job is upright, he should submit to God. God after all is in control of both nature and morality. We see here two strands of retribution which mingle in the poet's mind. He had been speaking of an almost automatic sequence of wrong-doing and misfortune, though we cannot be sure that underlying his words was no thought that God is the one who brings that affliction. Here he makes it plain that God is the one who directly brings the rain and reverses human circumstances, with the emphasis upon the punishment of the wicked. It is sometimes not entirely certain whether 'the poor' are simply those who are destitute. Often there are overtones of piety, as in many of the psalms and in the prayers of the pious in the countries outside of Israel. Sometimes the poor are those who are oppressed. Although he uses the same vocabulary as the other wisdom writers, our poet is often closer to the psalmists, and *the poor* in v. 16 seem to be those who are both pious and righteous and who have been down-trodden by the *unjust*. Since God is in ultimate control of the world, Eliphaz is saying, Job should appeal to him and plead for relief from his suffering.

5.17–18   Here we have a new idea, and one which will be taken up and expanded by Elihu: suffering is a discipline. If it is accepted as such God will restore the sufferer.

5.19–26 Having made the suggestion Eliphaz draws out with some exaggeration the return to happiness which follows such a true recognition of the pain and a right response to it. Here is a fine picture of the one who enjoys God's protection. (*Six* and *seven* in v. 19 are stock numbers expressing repeated deliverance; cf. Prov. 24.16; 30.15, 18, 21; Amos 1.6, 9, etc. for similar use of two numbers, the second one more than the first.) It might almost be a description of what it meant when the Satan said that God had *hedged* [Job] *round on every side with* [his] *protection* (1.10). He would be protected from harm, saved from starvation in time of famine and from harm in time of war, shielded from slander and violence, defended from wild animals; his fields will be free from stones (remember the rocky and barren hillsides of the countries of the Mediterranean coast), and his crops protected from depredations of wild animals. His whole household will be secure; he will have many children and grand-children; and at the end of a long life he will die in peace, like Moses, with all his faculties undimmed (Deut. 34.7; when there was no hope of any future life beyond the grave this was the highest blessing that could be conceived). It is all most attractive, with simile and metaphor to deck out the poetic images.

Although he is quite unaware of the divine wager, Eliphaz is telling Job to go on trusting God, even though disasters have befallen him. It may be discipline (though why the upright Job should need such a discipline is not clear). Let him hold on, however, and God will smile on him as before. In the end our poet fulfils this prediction. All is restored to Job, even twofold!

5.27 Eliphaz ends his speech by reaffirming the correctness of his theology and his understanding of life. He, as one of the wise men, has searched out the nature of human existence and has drawn upon the learning of those who came before him. Tradition and experience are the grounds of his assertions.

6–7 *Job's response*

One difficulty in reading the Old Testament in an English translation is that we use 'you' when addressing both one and several people and have only one imperative whether we are speaking to an individual or a crowd. Hebrew not only has singular and plural forms of every part of the verb but has different male and female forms. Every translation is far less precise than the original, therefore, and this often matters.

It is not immediately obvious to the English reader of this speech by Job that he is not addressing the friends for much of the time. Only by the time the reader reaches 7.12 does it begin to dawn that Job has turned away from the friends and is speaking directly to God. In fact the singular verbs begin at 7.7.

Once this is recognized further questions suggest themselves. At what point does Job break off his reply to the friends and begin to argue with God? Certainly by 7.7. But is he musing to himself in 7.1–6 or are these verses also directed to God? Probably Job's complaint begins with the new chapter, although the first six verses form a bridge from his response to the speech of Eliphaz to his angry words directed at God.

Turning back to the beginning of the speech, we find that there is a similar meditative introduction before the friends are personally addressed in 6.21, although vv. 14–20 point to them obliquely. Moreover the verbs from v. 21 are plural. It is plain even to the casual reader that in Job we do not have a Platonic dialogue in which argument is met with counter-argument and the course of the debate can be outlined and analysed. Indeed, so often do the speakers appear not to heed what has been said before their present statements that we might be tempted to feel that we are listening to a debate of the deaf. This is not entirely true, and some of the most recent commentators have drawn attention to links between the speeches which have tended to be overlooked in the past. Nevertheless we must not expect to find the to and fro of debate to which we are accustomed in the West. In several places Job addresses all three friends together, as here, rather than replying to the last speaker, or even appears to forget about them altogether in his anguish and his urgent desire to meet with God.

6.2–7 Job's initial response to Eliphaz is a return to his feelings which he expressed in ch. 3. It is no wonder that his words are *frenzied* when his misfortunes are so great. But there is a movement forward beyond that earlier outburst. He directly charges God with inflicting the distresses upon him: *The arrows of the Almighty find their mark in me.* Later Job's words will be yet more vehement. The sequence of thought is not entirely clear. Verse 5 echoes the ideas of vv. 2–3: how can he refrain from his complaining? If vv. 6–7 go together they would seem to continue the same theme of what is the natural response to some experience. On the other hand possibly v. 7 reflects Job's physical sufferings.

6.8–13 The longing for death to end it all is repeated in vv. 8–13. He will not commit suicide, but seeks God's final act of annihilation. The depth of his despair can be seen in his assertion that he would welcome extinction with leaps of joy. How can he summon up the strength and patience to endure any longer? Yet even in the midst of his moans he holds firmly to his innocence (v. 10c). This is one of the certain facts on which he will never waver or release his hold. To understand the book it is vital to keep in mind both Job's conviction of his own goodness, a goodness which God vouched for in his conversation with the Satan, and the depth of the suffering which has come upon him. Job is unwilling to admit any fault that merits such suffering, and since God is in control of the whole universe he will not allow God to escape the responsibility for what has happened to him.

6.14–21 Now Job is ready to respond to Eliphaz. But his approach is oblique. He speaks of the demands of friendship in a detached way. This is one of the longest and most elaborate images found in the book. To understand it we have to place ourselves in the fringes of Palestine, mountainous, rocky, desert for much of the year. The monsoon rains drain rapidly off the hillsides and fill the channels gouged out of the rock by centuries of these annual downpours. Only in the rainy season is there any water in these *watercourses*. Travellers coming across the real desert look for water in these intermittent streams. Perhaps in the past they had drunk from them and they press on eagerly as they draw closer to them. Great is their disappointment and despair when they find only a dried up wadi. 'You are as great a disappointment to me as that', says Job to his three friends.

6.22–23 He rounds on them. He had never made any demands upon them. He had never asked them to bail him out of financial difficulties or to provide a ransom for his release from those who had him in their power. It might seem that this is somewhat out of place in the dramatic setting of friends who had travelled long distances to offer comfort. Perhaps Job uses conventional phrases to express his sense of their failures in friendship.

6.24–30 In his final address to the friends Job accuses them of heartlessness. They have no proper sympathy with him, being alienated by his frenzied words which are natural from a man who has been afflicted as he has. Verse 30 is difficult, both in translation and meaning. If we follow REB Job denies that he has lost his sense of what is right and rejects the suggestion that he is so deranged that he is no longer responsible for what he says.

7.1–2 We have seen that 7.1–6 forms the transition from an address to the friends to a direct appeal to God. Probably these words are also to be taken as part of that appeal. Again Job moves from a general view to his own particular case. Human beings have a hard time of it. They are like slaves, forced to work in the blazing heat, or a day labourer whose wages have not been paid promptly at the end of the day and who has no other means of sustaining his life (cf. Deut. 24.15).

7.3–6 So Job feels himself to be. In a wonderfully evocative passage he describes his sufferings. How long the nights seem! His body is covered with sores in which worms breed. He is very aware of the brevity of human life – swifter than a weaver's shuttle flying across the warp, soon to come to an end like a thread that runs out from that shuttle.[1]

7.7–10 At last he speaks to God directly. His appeal is to God's understanding of his condition: *Remember*. Death is not far away. And death is final. The Babylonians spoke of the underworld as 'the land of no return', and Job picks up this picture. And his death will take place under the very eyes of God!

7.11–21 How then can he be silent? Yet when he speaks it is to utter fierce accusations against God. In the Psalms we catch glimpses of ancient stories in which God defeated primeval monsters and secured the permanence of the world by holding in check the mighty waters

---

[1] Compare the Babylonian sufferer's description of his illness, quoted in Appendix I.

(see Pss. 74.13–17; 93). Job asks whether God regards him as such a dangerous opponent that he has to *set a watch* over him. The picture of God which his sufferings have evoked is of a divine torturer: sleep might relieve his anguish – but God sends terrifying dreams to interrupt his rest. In a parody of Ps. 8 he portrays God as the divine spy. The Psalmist had found security in the thought that human beings are never beyond God's loving care. Job picks up the word that the Psalmist had used to describe God's continual watchful love over him, and uses it in its other meaning, punish. The divine spy never lets him out of his sight for a moment, always watching for his least fall into wrong-doing, always eager to inflict the punishment which has become a daily occurrence. What harm can any minor lapse cause to God? Why cannot God be magnanimous and let him off his punishment? He will soon die and his life will be at an end. Once that happens it will be too late. God may change his mind and start to look for him – but he will be no more, and the quest will be in vain.

Job's words are bitter and will get still harsher, yet they are important for our poet's design. This is what suffering does for a man, for the best of men. Suffering divides a man from his friends. Suffering erects a barrier between a man and his God. The one who suffers can only speak out frenzied words. How will the other friends react? What response can Job expect from God?

8 Bildad's first speech

Eliphaz was a religious man who combined piety with his experience of life and knowledge of traditional wisdom. Bildad trusts in the teaching passed down from earlier generations.

8.2–7 He is exasperated by Job's words – *long-winded ramblings of an old man*. God is utterly just, meting out retribution fairly and impartially. Reward and punishment are regular and exact. *If your sons sinned against him* he says, but means, 'Your sons were punished for some wrong-doing which they committed; no question about it.' So that when he points to Job himself his *if* contains more than a suspicion of doubt about Job's integrity. The reader remembers that two of the words which Bildad applies to Job were also used by God to describe his servant (*upright*, and *blameless* 1.8; 2.3). But if punishment always follows wrongdoing and only comes as a result of sin, then Job's fate indicates his character. At this point it is no more than a vague hint. Job's intransigence will lead the friends to draw the conclusion more forcefully. Relying upon past wisdom, Bildad picks up stock phrases and applies them to Job. There is no close link between *humble beginnings* and a *great* future in Job's case, except in the thought that if only he will submit to God he will be restored to his earlier prosperity.

8.8–10   At v. 8 Bildad discloses the foundation for his assertions: *Enquire now of older generations and consider the experience of their forefathers*. The lifetime of individuals is too short for them to arrive at any true understanding of the way God orders the world: *we are but of yesterday and know nothing*. Everyone must rely upon what earlier generations have discovered. This was very much in line with the practice of the wise men, who learnt and copied out the sayings of their predecessors.

8.11–19   He now sets out some of this teaching that he has acquired. Reeds and rushes need constant water at their roots, otherwise they will wither. So closely are cause and effect linked. REB links v. 13 with the following description of the spider's web, which becomes a simile for the confidence of the godless in their own security.[1] It may be, however, that v. 13 is the conclusion of the rush metaphor and applies the rapid withering of the reed to the destruction of the wicked. A third image is introduced in v. 16: the plant (is a weed intended?) which grows rapidly in a sunny garden, even though its roots have only stones to fasten onto (or possibly the meaning is that its roots twine firmly round the stones and give it added support). The gardener comes and pulls it up, however securely it seems to be established. The ground shows no concern for it once it has been rooted out and other plants quickly take its place.

8.20–22   At the end of his speech Bildad repeats his main asssertion: reward and goodness, punishment and evil-doing are intimately linked. Therefore Job can be reassured that he will soon enjoy once more his earlier happiness. And again Bildad cannot reach beyond

[1] The same word translated 'life-thread' is found here as in 7.6. In both places REB offers 'hope', the more common meaning of the word, as an alternative. 'Thread' (if the Hebrew can bear it) suits the context, as well as providing a link between Job's and Bildad's speeches.

stock phrases and familiar lore, and even while he addresses Job directly his words are generalized proverbial wisdom.

9–10   *Job turns away from his friends*

Bildad has set out the traditional theology, often in well-worn phrases. It is perhaps little wonder, therefore, that Job does not reply directly. He too accepts this view of divine retribution. That is his problem. He is confident that he has not committed any sin that merits so heavy a punishment, yet he believes in a God who rules the world justly, apportioning rewards to those whose lives are upright and punishing those who have committed evil. What has gone wrong? It is not a matter of refuting Bildad's theology, for it is similar to his own. He can only try to make some sense of the contradiction between his life and his theology. In the end it will be his theology which has to yield. But he has a more immediate concern.

If he is blameless and God is just, what is needed is to present his case to God. Yet will this secure his acquittal? It is an issue which troubles him beyond this present speech.

9.2–3   He begins from an awareness of God's immense power. If anyone were to try to argue his case against God, God could simply refuse to answer.

9.4–10   This leads into a description of God's supremacy over nature. We need to remember the Israelite picture of the world. Lacking modern knowledge of the universe, the Israelites' conceptions were akin to those in Babylon and were derived from what we actually see around us. The earth is a flat plate, supported on pillars, with the solid dome of the sky over it, the whole surrounded by the waters of the primeval deep. Sun, moon and stars move across the dome. God was the creator and still controls all the natural phenomena. Our poet and the writer of Genesis 1 have a similar cosmology (see also Pss. 24.1–2; 75.3). According to other ideas, God had to overcome the forces of chaos before he could produce the ordered world, and this is alluded to in v. 8, where the *sea monster* is probably imagined in much the same way as Tiamat in the Babylonian creation story or

Yam, against whom Baal fought.[1] A little later Job mentions *Rahab*, another of the opponents vanquished by God (see Ps. 89.10; Isa. 51.9). While, however, the writer of Genesis and the Psalmists concentrate upon the beneficial activities of God in imposing order upon chaos, Job sees chiefly his irrational and destructive actions, overturning the mountains, producing earthquakes, forbidding the sun from rising, shutting up the stars so that they cannot shine. Although he *does great, unsearchable things, marvels beyond all reckoning*, the emphasis is on God's immense power and the impossibility of human beings ever understanding him, or being able to resist him.

9.11–24   It is impossible even to make contact with such a God, still

[1] The account in *Enuma Elish* is well known. Marduk arms himself and fights Tiamat. (Trans. by E. A. Speiser, *ANET* (see p. xii above), p. 67.)

> Then joined issue Tiamat and Marduk, wisest of gods.
> They swayed in single combat, locked in battle.
> The lord spread out his net to enfold her,
> The Evil Wind, which followed behind, he let loose in her face.
> When Tiamat opened her mouth to consume him,
> He drove in the Evil Wind that she close not her lips.
> As the fierce winds charged her belly,
> Her body was distended and her mouth was wide open.
> He released the arrow, it tore her belly,
> It cut through her insides, splitting the heart.
> Having thus subdued her, he extinguished her life.
> He cast down her carcass to stand upon it. . . .
>
> He split her like a shellfish into two parts:
> Half of her he set up and ceiled it as sky,
> Pulled down the bar and posted guards.
> He bade them to allow not her waters to escape.

At Ugarit Baal is fitted out with two clubs, 'Driver' and 'Expeller', and goes into battle.

> The club danced from the hand of Baal,
> [like] an eagle from his fingers.
> It struck the crown of prince [Yam],
> between the eyes of judge Nahar.
> Yam collapsed (and) fell to the earth;
> his joints quivered
> and his form crumpled.
> Baal dragged out Yam and laid him down,
> he made an end of judge Nahar.

The shout then goes up:

> Yam is indeed dead! Baal shall be king!

(Trans. by J. C. L. Gibson, *Canaanite Myths and Legends*, T. & T. Clark 1978, pp. 44–45 less to require of him an explanation of his doings. How then can Job plead his cause? If summoned to a court, God would not answer Job's accusation. He is too powerful for anyone to compel him to put in an appearance. And then Job flings aside all reserve and describes how this all-powerful being seems to him. He rains blows on him *without cause* (it was what God told the Satan he had incited him to do, 2.3). He twists his words so that he is led to condemn himself. He knows he is *blameless* yet makes him out to be *crooked*. And broadening out his accusation, he asserts: *He destroys blameless and wicked alike*. This mighty God has overturned all distinctions between good and evil, and instead of being the benign deity who allows men and women to enjoy their lives, which end all too rapidly in death, he destroys them all, he even *mocks the plight of the innocent*. Still there is more. God hands the land into the power of the wicked and *blindfolds the eyes of its judges*, so that they no longer protect the innocent and condemn the guilty. It is an outburst which comes very near to that cursing of God to his face which the Satan predicted Job would do if the blessings with which God had surrounded him were stripped away. REB has deleted a short section at the end of v. 24, *if not he, then who?* (see mg.). The words may not be the later comment of a scribe, as the translators suppose, and although they disturb the poetic line this is perhaps intentional. Job is unwilling to let God off the hook. Who else but he can possibly be responsible for this disordered world? He is the mighty creator. In the end he must take responsibility for the way the world is.

9.25–32 From his survey of the world, condemned to violence, injustice, and pain, Job turns once more to his own brief existence. His days have slipped away as swiftly as a runner, a light skiff skimming across the water, or a vulture swooping down on its prey. Attempts to raise his spirits are vain. He *knows* that God will condemn him in the end. Even if he admitted that he was in the wrong and undertook an elaborate cleansing rite, God would thrust him back into the mire. The sudden change to *you* in v. 31 is striking. So far he has been speaking of God in the third person, and he will return to this in the rest of the chapter. It is as if he cannot avoid a direct address to God, so intense is his longing to present his case to him and to meet him face to face.

9.33–35 With such a powerful God there is only one hope – an arbitrator to mediate between them. Such a mediator, however, would have to be greater than God himself, one able to impose his authority upon them both. It is an empty hope. No one is greater than God. *If Only . . .*[2]

But if there were such an umpire, if it were possible to arraign God, what would he say? The next chapter sets out the plea that Job would make.

10.2 *Do not condemn me, but let me know the charge against me.* This will resound throughout the rest of the book, for Job will not abandon his certainty that he is blameless. If only he could get through to God on equal terms, he is certain that he would be able to vindicate himself.

10.3–7 Without such an opportunity, God's treatment of him is nothing other than *oppression*. God's omniscience and almighty power make his torture even more reprehensible. He is not limited as humans are. He knows that Job is guiltless. He also knows that he is free to continue his persecution, for there is no one able to deliver Job out of his hands.[3]

10.8–17 Yet those were the very hands which made him. Does God not see what he is doing? His hands created Job, moulding him from the clay (cf. Gen. 2.7). Is he really prepared to use those same hands to reduce him to dust again? It is so incomprehensible that Job sets up a scenario that is itself beyond reason. God made him through an infinitely wonderful process in his mother's womb (cf. Ps. 139.13–16). He cared for him up to the moment the disaster struck. And behind all that care was a secret purpose – to catch him out in some sin and then mount this onslaught upon him? And it would make no difference whether he had lived an upright life or not.

10.18–22 A frequent cry of the afflicted in the Psalms is 'Why?' To this Job now comes. Why did God ever bring him out of the womb and give him life? Life itself is short. Beyond the grave there is only the land of dust and darkness and forgetfulness, the land from which

---

[2] I find the final line of ch. 9 quite inexplicable in REB. The Hebrew literally reads, 'For not so (*or* just) I with me.' There have been many emendations. The boldest, and perhaps on that account the correct one, since it suits the mood of Job is, 'For he is not just with me.'

[3] The questions which Job asks are, of course, impossible. God does not have only human eyes, unable to distinguish between saint and sinner. He is not restricted to a human life-span, so that he must hastily punish Job even before he is guilty lest he slip through his hands.

there is no return. Why then will not God allow him a few brief moments of happiness, instead of inflicting the torture?

In his response to Eliphaz Job had drawn the picture of the divine spy, constantly on the lookout to catch him out in some wrongdoing. Now he has presented the image of the divine torturer whose apparent care for him was with a fell intent. Because he knows he is blameless, God's treatment of him can only mean that God is indifferent to right and wrong. There is no justice in the running of the universe. God may not worry about this, but to Job it is of supreme importance. He will not abandon his integrity. He will not let go of his demand for a justly ordered world. And yet he cannot give up his deep longing to meet with God – even this God that he has now portrayed. Here we begin to see something of the greatness of our poet, whose daring reaches beyond anything that we find in the whole Bible.

11   Zophar speaks

Zophar is depicted as the lest sympathetic of the three friends. So certain is he of the exact correspondence of morality and a man's fortune that he is convinced that Job must be a sinner because he has suffered so great punishment. Job's questioning appears nothing less than blasphemy, and his response is as much an attempt to silence Job as to bring him comfort or offer guidance.

11.2–3   His first sentence reveals his sense of outrage. Job's speeches are a *spate of words*, he possesses a *glib tongue*, his talk is *endless*. Such irreverence must be rebuked.

11.4–6   The rebuke is fierce and brutal: the punishment which God is inflicting is less than Job's sin deserves! Although he professes to be quoting Job, Job has never exactly said to God, *I am spotless in your sight*. The words broadly represent Job's attitude. He holds firmly to his integrity, but it was Bildad who had applied the word *spotless* to him (8.6, REB *pure* – Job will later say that his prayer is *sincere*, 16.17, the same Hebrew word). So Zophar longs for a more direct revelation from God, that will silence Job. *Wisdom* includes both the principles upon which the universe is founded and God's moral rule. We notice that although Zophar stresses the mystery of God, he is confident that he knows exactly how God governs the world and bluntly passes judgment on Job.

11.7–12 Having condemned Job as a great sinner, Zophar reverts to his description of the greatness of God's knowledge and power. No one can attain any understanding of him, for he is beyond the reach of heaven and earth, the underworld and the sea. No searching will discover his secrets, and there is no one who can reverse his decisions. Such a mighty and all-seeing God can certainly search out the iniquity of men's hearts – with the implication that he knows exactly what hidden sins Job has committed. Verse 12 is apparently a proverb, the precise meaning of which is far from clear. Apparently our poet placed it in Zophar's mouth at this point as a further swipe at Job – ignorant as well as evil. The fool is the hollow man, the one without sense or moral principle.

11.13–20 Pious exhortation follows. Since Job has clearly been shown to be a great sinner by the punishments that have been laid upon him, he should turn back to God in prayer and thrust the evil from him. Let him repent and amend his life. Then God's blessing will return to him. His troubles will be forgotten, he will have the confidence of God's protection, and, in a phrase which Micah also uses to express complete security and peace of mind, Job will *lie down unafraid* (Micah 4.4). But if Job refuses to repent. . . ? Zophar ends his exhortation with a grim reminder that God will not allow the wicked to go unpunished. How different is the *hope* of the penitent from that of the sinner. The one has the hope of divine *protection* and will have no fear: the only hope that the other can grasp at is *death*, his only escape from his sufferings (cf. vv. 18 and 20).

It is curious that Zophar can paint such a lively picture of the mystery of God, whose ways are unsearchable, and yet can be so confident that he knows exactly how God rules the world and precisely how sin and punishment are matched in the life of Job. Our poet had a keen sense of the dangers of a too confident and too dogmatic faith.

12–14   *Job's response at the end of the first round of speeches*

Job's speech at the end of this first cycle is longer than any of his other utterances except the last. In some ways it marks a decisive stage in the argument. The friends have set out their arguments, and their lack of understanding, for all their initial sympathy with Job, has become plain. Job and they stand on opposite sides, not only in debate but also in their attitudes to God and their relations with him. Already, despite his rebellion and the frenzied talk that comes close to blasphemy, it is Job who is seen as the truly religious man. We need to watch the way in which this develops as the dialogue proceeds.

The speech is complex, with shifts from the opening address to the friends collectively to a short section where Job speaks to a single friend, on to sections that are close to musing, and finally a direct and agonized prayer to God. Again the English pronouns and verbs conceal some of these changes and it will be necessary to look closely at the text itself.

12.2–6   Incensed by their claim to superior knowledge, Job protests his equality with them in knowledge and wisdom. Sarcasm creeps into his words. When the friends die *wisdom will perish* with them! He complains that in spite of his understanding and discernment, he is treated with mockery. We may pick out three features in his plea that will be important for interpreting the whole book. First, he reaffirms that he is *innocent* and *blameless*, words that have already been seen to be important in his declarations of his upright life and character. Whatever else must be jettisoned, Job will never let go of his consciousness that he has committed no sin that would merit such suffering as he has had to endure. Second, he repeats what he senses to be the accusation of those who observe his misfortunes: he *called upon God* and yet God *afflicted* him. Those who held fast to the traditional theology would see God's failure to intervene in the face of Job's sufferings as further evidence that Job must be guilty of some hidden sin. The silence of God appears to condemn him. And because Job holds the same basic theology as the friends this increases his perplexity and pain. Third, Job yet again widens the area of debate: while all this has been happening to an innocent man, others whose crimes are blatant and who pay no heed to God are *left undisturbed* and *live safe and sound*. Whether we call it the problem of suffering or

29

rather see it as the enigma of God's rule, this must surely have been a matter of deep concern to our poet.[1]

12.7–10   There is no easy way out of the dilemma, for Job believes in a God who is all powerful and in whose sole control the whole world rests. Nature acknowledges this. So God is responsible for all that happens to men and women.[2]

12.11–12   Verses 11–12 are difficult. They appear to go with the section of Job's speech that we have just read, but they follow awkwardly. What is the meaning of the question about the ear testing words? Perhaps Job is asserting his right to exercise his own judgment rather than meekly accepting traditional wisdom and so to reject the arguments of the friends. In v. 12 Job repeats traditional learning and pushes it aside. Again he appears to be setting his own critical discernment against the teaching on which the friends rely.[3]

12.13–15   Were it not for the stress upon the destructiveness of God, the next section might well be taken for a hymn in praise of God's power. Perhaps it is based on such a psalm.[4] But in Job's mouth it is twisted into a fierce arraignment of God for the cruel use he makes of his omnipotence. He *pulls down, imprisons*, produces drought and devastating flood, destroys the reason of counsellors, judges and priests, and makes kings powerless. He *leads people astray and destroys them*, leaving them without effective rulers. We have already seen that Job does not flinch from placing blame for all natural and human disasters upon God. Here his parody of a hymn of praise makes us again ask, If this is how things really are, what kind of a God is the master of the universe?[5]

13.1–12   The friends had claimed that their doctrine was based upon

[1] One possible rendering of the final line of v. 6 is given in the margin, placed there because REB found it unintelligible. The meaning may be that the wicked men who are described in this verse feel that they wield the power of God and so have no need of him.

[2] The address in vv. 7–8 is singular. Job appears to turn to one of the friends.

[3] REB prints v. 12 as a quotation, but also adds a question mark. What seems to be needed for the sense is one or the other.

[4] Throughout these verses Job never once says 'God' but always 'He' (REB has inserted 'God' in v. 13 to make the sense clear).

[5] The quotation marks in v. 13 are strange. Presumably REB interprets the verse as a further quotation of traditional lore, or, as is suggested above, it comes from a hymn of praise. Job would then be seen as picking up a phrase from a well known teaching or liturgy and developing it in the bitter way that has been indicated.

their own experience. Job counters this by asserting that he has personal knowledge of the events he has just described and knows that this is how God acts. Nevertheless, he still wishes to talk with this malevolent God. The friends have tried to defend God by uttering falsehoods about him. Job asserts that God does not wish to have what is not true set out in his defence. This is one of the most striking passages in the whole book. On the one hand we have the friends, totally convinced of the truth of their theology, so certain that God can allege not only that Job has done wrong but that he merits even greater punishment than he has received. On the other side stands Job, unshakeable in his knowledge that he has committed no crime worthy of such suffering, and so distraught that he can see only the disasters that afflict mankind, and so honest with himself that he does not flinch from describing the kind of being God must be who brings these disasters upon the world he has created. And yet it is not the friends who pray to God but Job.

13.13–19   Before he addresses God Job has a final word to say to the friends. He is going to take up God's challenge boldly. Whatever God chooses to inflict upon him he will not abandon his certainty of his innocence but will defend his conduct to God's face. It is strange that he retains sufficient confidence in God's integrity, in spite of all he has just said, that he can affirm, *once I have stated my case I know that I shall be acquitted*. Partly it is the gamble of a man who has nothing to lose. The worst that can happen will be that God kills him. Yet trust is stronger than despair. No godless person can get near to God, so that if he can manage to find his way to the divine tribunal his case is as good as won.[6]

13.20–27   So Job addresses God?[7] The *two conditions* which Job demands are probably set out in v. 21. Job asks God to *remove* his *hand* from upon him (i.e. to stop torturing him) and to terrify him no longer. Then, he says, he will be prepared either to state his case or to reply to God's accusations. Having begun to speak, however, he

---

[6] Although it is not my intention to comment on textual problems, the AV translation of v. 15 is so striking that it cannot be passed by. How many sermons must have been preached on, 'Though he slay me, yet will I trust in him'? This does not suit the context, where Job is challenging God, not trusting in him. There are two forms of the Hebrew, which can be translated: 'Behold, he will slay me; I have no hope' (so RSV), and 'Though he slay me, yet will I wait for him' (so RV). It is not clear how REB arrived at its translation. Is it a paraphrase of the more literal RSV?

[7] God has been added in REB to make this clear.

continues with a violent arraignment of God. Why has God become his enemy? Why is he being punished for the indiscretions of his youth? Why is he being treated like a criminal, one who must be kept under constant surveillance, a slave branded who, if he runs away, can be easily caught? The boldness of Job's words is astonishing.

14.1–6   In a more measured tone, Job proceeds to present his plea. It is an elaborate exposition of the brevity of human life, which is so short that it is heartless of God to pursue an individual so vindictively, especially when it is God himself, the creator, who has set the limit to the length of his existence.[8]

14.7–12   How different is the life of a tree, which will sprout again even when it is cut down. But when a mortal dies he will never rise again. Never can he be roused from that final sleep. We cannot feel the full pressure of Job's sufferings until we come to an appreciation of this. Christians have to put aside the resurrection hope if they are to understand the book of Job. Classical ideas of the immortality of the soul have combined with Christian belief, and for centuries the dominant thought has been that the life of each individual continues beyond the grave. It comes as a shock to realize that for most of the Old Testament period this life was held to be all. It is important to pay close attention to this section of Job's complaint. The rise of humanism, however, and a general secularizing of Western society makes it somewhat easier for us in this century to enter sympathetically into Job's world. For many of our contemporaries death is as final as it was for Job.

14.13–16 There is no real hope of a future life in the book, and yet our poet presents Job as longing for such a future as he turns to speak directly to God at 14.13. *If only. . .* ! It is an empty hope he knows. Even his longing is hemmed in by his certainty that death is final. His impossible yearning is that God would hide him in Sheol and *fix a time* when he would think once more of his loyal servant and recall him. Sheol then would be a refuge rather than a place of destruction. Job cannot understand why God has become his enemy. It must be because he is angry with his servant. But anger will pass and God

---

[8] REB has transposed two verses in this chapter (13.28 to follow 14.2 and 14.14a to the middle of v. 12); 14.4 is relegated to the margin, presumably because it was felt that the theme of the passage is of the shortness of human life not human sinfulness. The other verses fit more easily in their new positions, but this may be Western prejudice.

will once again *long to see* the being he has made with such loving care. His mood would have changed. Instead of watching his every action to catch him out in some sin, God would call and eagerly Job would answer. If only this could be so he would not lose hope, even in Sheol. Like a soldier on guard he would wait to be relieved from his post.

14.17–22   But Job knows that it is wishful thinking. God stores up his every sinful action in order to punish him. Death is the end. The all-powerful deity will finally banish him out of his sight and he will be destroyed. In Sheol there is no remembrance. Whatever fortune awaits his sons, whether they rise to places of honour in their community or sink into lowly obscurity, he will remain in ignorance, aware of nothing. Job's final words speak of the grief which the dead man's relatives and slaves feel at his departing. Does our poet wish us to see a contrast between the sorrow which even slaves feel for their master and the anger of God who has *wiped out the hope of frail man?*

15   Eliphaz describes the distress of the wicked

Eliphaz has become noticeably harsher in the face of Job's refusal to accept his suffering as divine discipline. He criticizes Job for his lack of piety and then enters on a long account of the fate of the wicked.

15.2–6   Job's outbursts show that he is not truly wise. *Hot-air arguments* admirably presents the sense of Eliphaz's words in a modern idiom, but to grasp the full meaning of the metaphor in the next line we have to remember that in Palestine the *east wind* is the hot, dust-laden wind that blows in from the desert. Eliphaz goes further with his accusations: Job has thrown off all reverence and denounced God. All *communication* with him is at an end. Dogma has now distorted reality. To Eliphaz Job's blasphemous words show that he is ungodly and profane. He has cut himself off from God. In truth Job alone among the group of disputants ever addresses God direct. For all his unbridled utterance, he longs for God with a desire that the friends can never understand.

15.7–10   Job had claimed that he was no less wise than the friends.

Eliphaz reverses this and goes beyond it. They are endowed with *insight* no less than he. Living at a time when only the latest invention is prized and it is the young who are credited with skills of innovation and expertise, while early retirement is required of those who are deemed to have outlived their usefulness, we have to make a leap of understanding in order to appreciate the meaning of Eliphaz's reference to *age and white hairs*. Eliphaz declares what would have been universally accepted at that time. As older men they possess the understanding that comes with age. The reference to the *firstborn of mankind* is probably a reminiscence of an old-world account of the first man, the primeval human being who was credited with wisdom that surpassed that of any of his later descendants (cf. 38.21). Again we need to transfer our ways of thinking to a time when the golden age lay in the past and history marked a persistent decline from early enlightened times.

15.11–13   It is not entirely clear how Eliphaz thinks of the *consolation from God*. REB seems to relate the revelation to Eliphaz's earlier account of his night vision (4.16), although the vocabulary used is quite different. Perhaps he still believes that he and the other friends are bringing this comforting word to Job. Whatever the means through which God speaks to him, Eliphaz can only regard Job's outbursts as blameworthy.

15.14–16   There is certainly a flashback to the vision in vv. 14–16, where Eliphaz reiterates the message he had then received. No human being is *innocent*. Not even the heavenly beings are pure. And to strengthen his case he overstates it: far from being pure, humans are *loathsome and corrupt* and *lap up evil like water*. It is probably unnecessary to point out that *justified* in v. 14 carries none of the overtones with which a Pauline theology has endowed it. The reference is to the innocent man who is acquitted in a court of law.

15.17–35   Having libelled Job, Eliphaz can see no other way of presenting his case against him than by trotting out the well-worn theology that Job's experience has effectively demolished. He repeats his earlier claims. Both his own knowledge and time-honoured lore agree that the wicked man will suddenly meet his punishment. More, he suggests that the wicked never enjoy peace of mind but all their days are *racked with anxiety*. Varied pictures are evoked to bring this vividly before Job: the sudden attack by a marauding band, death by an enemy's sword followed by the swoop of the vultures upon his corpse. He will suffer the distress of a king about to be toppled from his throne. His home city will be laid in ruins, his house left a heap of rubble, his wealth carried off. The irreligious blasphemer is compared to a tree the shrivels from its roots, a vine that sheds its unripened grapes, an olive whose blossom drops without bearing fruit. Metaphor and description rush in a mingled flurry of words, many of them impossible to represent in the English translation, as Eliphaz hastens on to convince Job of the truth of traditional teaching.

It is a depressing speech. The kindliest of the friends is out of his depth. He has based his life upon his own experience, enriched by a special revelation, and upon the learning that has come down from the past and which he has spent a lifetime mastering. It does not fit Job's case. So much the worse. It must be Job who is in the wrong. The teaching is indisputable. All that needs to be done is to convince Job of its truth.

16–17 Job's fluctuating moods

16.2–3 Job picks up the Hebrew word translated *mischief* at the end of Eliphaz's speech and turns it back against the friends. They are *trouble-makers*. REB suggests that the next two sentences are quotations of a kind, reflecting what they are saying or thinking, and we may look to the beginning of the speech which Eliphaz has just made for examples of these ideas.

16.4–5 To this Job responds by saying that if he were in their place he could easily *harangue* them as they have lectured him. *But no*, were he the one who had come to visit a friend in distress, he would offer *condolences* and *encouragement*, instead of their hard words.

16.6–10 Then he bitterly complains about their failure. His suffering continues, yet his friends have become his enemies. The exact meaning of the Hebrew is not readily discerned. REB has inserted *my friend* and interprets vv. 7–9 as a description of the impact that the friends' words have had upon Job.[1] They come against him in fierce

---

[1] I wonder whether this is correct. May not these verses have been addressed to God?

anger rather than as companions seeking to soothe his anguish. They have ganged up against him to assail him with taunts.

16.11–14   Even God has become his enemy, leaving him *at the mercy of malefactors*, and then striking at him himself. The image of v. 12ab is of the attack by a wild animal. In the next line the figure changes, and God is depicted as a warrior who has made Job his target. It is a bitter and harsh picture and recalls chs. 7 and 9.

16.15–17   Wearing sackcloth was a sign of repentance and mourning (cf. Jonah 3.5–8; Gen. 37.34; II Sam 3.31). Job certainly does not intend any confession of sin, for, as he says in v. 17, he has not committed any violent crimes and his prayer has been *sincere* (it is the word translated *pure* in 8.6 and *sound* in 11.4, there spoken by Bildad and Zophar, but truly representing Job's own conviction). Rather it appears to be a sign of humility and expression of his sufferings, linked with incessant *weeping*.

16.18–17.1   Suddenly his mood changes. He cries aloud for vindication. Abel's blood cried out to God from the ground (Gen. 4.10), and Job pleads for justice for his death at the hands of God. Yet his appeal is to God against God. His words are wild. There must be a *witness in heaven*, and REB sees this witness as none other than God himself. Job appeals to God, still unable to believe that he will not find justice, though he turns *anxiously* to him. Yet God has proved his enemy. *If only there were one to arbitrate between man and God.* REB finds here a renewed longing for a mediator, which we noted earlier in 9.33, and sees Job drawing a parallel between this arbitrator between God and himself and the umpire who decides between men who in dispute. The need is urgent. Again the thought of his imminent death hovers over all his pleading. His days are numbered. There is no return along the road he is travelling.

17.2–5   This speech of Job is a masterpiece of poetic craft. Seldom have the fluctuating moods of the sufferer been so well depicted. Desire for a mediator is now replaced by a direct appeal to God. Feeling that he will get nothing but mockery from his human friends, Job turns to the only one who remains, the God who a moment ago was seen as his enemy, pitilessly raining his arrows at him. He cannot bring himself to believe that this God has utterly abandoned justice. All comes from God and God is responsible for everything that happens in the world. *You will not let those triumph whose minds you have sunk in ignorance.*

17.6–8   Again his mood changes and he returns to self-pity. He is held up as a *byword*. His fate has *bewildered* the upright. Is this an oblique plea to God to reassert his justice? By allowing his righteous servant to suffer in this way God has undermined the confidence of the *upright* and the *innocent*. Trust in God's government of the world is imperilled. Goodness is compromised. Faith is threatened.

17.9–10   Yet Job will not abandon *his* integrity. Despite appearances, although it seems that God has changed into an unjust and cruel tyrant, even if he receives no justice, the one who knows he is righteous will hold firmly to his integrity.

17.11–16   In the end despair appears to triumph. The precise sense is obscure in one or two places, as the margin indicates, but the general drift is plain. Death stands darkly before Job. Sheol will be his house, his bed will be made in darkness, the grave and the worm will be his nearest kin, and into that gloomy land from which there is no return he cannot take either his *hope* in God or his *piety*.

18   Bildad sets out the fate of the wicked

After condemning Job's complaints and telling him to be silent, Bildad describes the fate which will meet the wicked. It is little more than a recapitulation of the traditional theology, filled out with a range of images and poetic devices.

18.2–4   Bildad is irritated by Job's confidence that he is in the right and resents the way he has rejected the arguments of the friends out of hand. Job had used the phrase 'a rock is dislodged from its place' to indicate the ruthless way God had inflicted the sufferings upon him (14.18). Bildad repeats the exact phrase, here translated *or the rocks to be moved from their place*, but in a completely different sense. Will God bring about these violent changes in nature simply to prove Job right? It is unreasonably for him to expect that God will order things just for his own satisfaction.

18.5–6 Now follows one of the most extensive accounts of divine retribution. Eliphaz had described the fears for the future that terrify the wicked, as well as setting out the way in which they would be suddenly destroyed (ch. 15). Bildad elaborates on the disasters which will come upon them.

In an age when starting a fire was more difficult than striking a safety match, it was normal to keep a light permanently burning. A lamp became a symbol of well-being. The lamp of the wicked will be extinguished.

18.7–10 With six different words for a snare, Bildad then depicts the evil man being caught in a trap.

18.11–16 Fear of death suddenly overcomes such a man. He is stricken by disease and taken away to the realm of the dead. *Death's firstborn* and *death's terrors* may have been demons, or they may be poetic images. Fire destroys his home. Like a tree he withers and dies.

18.7–19 In a world where there was no hope of a future life of bliss, a man's survival was seen in the continuance of his name and the lives of his children. The name of the wicked is forgotten and he leaves no descendants. Thus he is totally annihilated.

Bildad ends by describing the horror with which those living in the west and east hear of the fate of such a man.

18.20–21 For all his dogmatism, Bildad shows little reverence for God. It is as if the retribution is expected to follow automatically, and God is only mentioned in the last verse of the chapter. Not only does Bildad show little sensitivity to Job's distress, he is essentially irreligious, for all his emphasis upon the punishment of evil-doers. All we find in this chapter is a stern theology passionately defended.

19 Job's plea for vindication

This is one of the most important speeches by Job and contains the well known but immensely difficult passage which has been of great comfort to the dying and bereaved, and which cannot now be separated from Handel's music, 'I know that my redeemer liveth'. It will need an even greater effort to strip off these Christian overtones and get back to our poet.

19.2–12 Job's initial response to Bildad is to complain about his treatment by the friends. Their advice increases his grief and crushes him. They have wronged him by their accusations of some sin which is the reason for his punishment. Verse 4 does not seem to fit very well with Job's convictions. He is confident of his innocence, and it is not a question of his sin being a private matter between him and his God. His complaint against the friends is that they are hostile to him, not that they interfere. Perhaps Job means that even if he had committed some evil he has not injured them. The verse may reveal his desire to meet God face to face and be done with these troublesome friends. This last interpretation would prepare us for the question which follows. It is not the friends who are his real accusers and torturers. God has *drawn his net* round him, *blocked* his *path, stripped* him *of all honour*, destroyed him like an uprooted tree, attacked him as an invading army besieges a walled town. No one answers his cries for help. God to whom he has appealed has become his enemy. Here is to be found the depth of his distress. The God who had been his friend and who had hedged him round with his protecting love seems to have changed his character. It makes no sense – but Job will not give up the certainty that he is innocent. Justice is what he demands, and will not abandon the quest.

19.13–20 His sense of outrage at what God has done to him leads Job to describe yet again his evil plight. Everyone shuns him. Relatives and friends have turned away. His servants and slaves have lost all respect for him and will not obey his orders, even when he pleads with them. He is estranged from his wife. Even children *turn their backs* on him (and we need to keep in mind the respect for age which has been instilled into them from their youngest years). His body has wasted away until he is no more than skin and bones.[1]

19.21–22 With great pathos, Job appeals once again to his friends. Why are they treating him in the same way that God does? When he faces the divine enemy, surely they can pity him. It has been

---

[1] Although v. 20b in the AVB has become proverbial: 'I am escaped with the skin of my teeth', it is difficult to see precisely what the words can mean and many interpretations and emendations have been proposed. REB adopts a mixture of emendation and new meanings to provide a description of Job's anguish at his diseased and afflicted state.

well said, 'The whole tragedy of the book is packed into these extraordinary words. Job's complaint of his friends is that they are too God-like. What higher ideal can men have than the imitation of God? And yet their conduct may be most inhuman just when it seems to them most divine.'[2]

19.23–27b   The annihilation of death looms before Job. He has no hope of a return to his former happy life. All that is left to him is the desperate longing for vindication. He first looks for a permanent record of his declarations of innocence – inscribed in a rock, the letters filled with lead to ensure that they will not become illegible. And then he makes a gigantic leap of faith. The universe cannot be utterly unjust. He will be vindicated. And he will know that he has been cleared of these false accusations of wrongdoing. This much is plain. What is far from obvious is the exact meaning of the Hebrew, and since this is such a central passage and REB has moved so far from the familiar translations it is necessary for once to comment on the text.

The problems are partly questions of the meaning of the words, partly matters of textual corruption. In places the Hebrew yields no sense, and every translation has made some alterations in the text. The difficulties are increased because of the theological sensitiveness of the passage, and interpreters tend either to read in or emend out the hope of life after death, largely according to their preconceived ideas.

'Redeemer' certainly bears the wrong overtones. The word is heavily weighted with Christian ideas. Moreover the idea of 'saviour' does not accord with what Job is seeking. He is not looking for someone who will lift him from his present sufferings. What he is demanding is vindication of his innocence.[3]

The second line reads literally, 'And a later one (or last one) will arise upon dust.' The 'later one' is the vindicator, and 'dust' may be either the ground or, less probably, Job's grave or Sheol. REB seems to have regarded the gate of the city, where the elders met to administer justice, as a dusty place, hence *in court*. The point about speaking last is that the last speaker was expected to win the case.

The next line is almost unintelligible: 'and after my skin they strip

[2] Strahan, *The Book of Job Interpreted*, p. 174.
[3] The Hebrew word means the next of kin on whom the duty falls to buy back land that has been sold outside of the family and to carry out blood revenge in cases of murder (cf. Lev. 25.26, 33; Num. 35.9–28; Deut. 19.1–13; II Sam. 14.4–11; Ruth 2.20; 3.9, 12; 4.1–8; Jer. 32.6–15).

off this' (fem. and so with no immediate word to which it refers), and naturally there have been a multitude of emendations. REB adopts slight changes to 'and after' and 'my skin' to produce *I shall discern my witness*, and apparently introduces further emendations to produce a line which accords with its overall picture of a law court situation. Those who think that Job believes that he will be vindicated after his death accept some such meaning as 'after my skin has been struck off'.

REB continues the court scene in the following line, which is ambiguous but easily translatable as either 'and from within my flesh' (i.e. while I am still alive) or 'and away from my flesh' (apart from the body, as a spirit after death) 'I shall see God'. The problem is what precise meaning to give to the preposition before 'flesh'. These translations accord with the view of a vindication either during or after Job's lifetime. REB continues the court scene, finding *my defending counsel* in the Hebrew word 'from my flesh'.

Job says that he will *see* his vindication, either because he is still alive, or although he is in Sheol. Since he appears to anticipate his death in vv. 23–24 and earlier he has cried for his blood to demand vindication (16.18), it seems most likely that he is hoping for a momentary release from the forgetfulness of the land of the dead so that he can know that his innocence has been vindicated at last.

We should probably not press the court scene too far and ask who is the judge if God is the defending counsel and vindicator. If we wish for a consistency which is alien to poetry it will be necessary to abandon the REB translation, at least in v. 26.

19.27c–29   REB takes the last line of v. 27 as the introduction to Job's final warning to the friends. Again the text is difficult and the exact meaning is uncertain, but REB produces a reasonable sense. The friends point to the *misfortunes* which have befallen Job and claim that this shows that he is guilty of some secret sin. This certainly fits the general tenor of the dialogue, although it requires emending the Hebrew. Job then warns them that despite all appearances there is a righteous judge who will condemn them for their false condemnation of him.

It is disheartening to discover that well-loved passages of scripture almost certainly do not mean what we have long taken them to mean, but honesty forbids avoiding the consequences of a careful study of the text. Even if the Christian overtones of the 'redeemer' passage have to be abandoned, our poet reaches great heights of spiritual perception in this chapter. He sensitively presents the anguish which

41

the friends have inflicted upon the one whose sufferings initiated the dialogue. He vividly depicts Job's pitiable condition, abandoned by friends, an alien to his nearest remaining family. His account of the court scene in which Job hopes against all appearances for vindication is almost as memorable in its new dress as it was in the old. Finally, Job's appeal to the friends to show pity and cease persecuting him in the way that God is doing, and his warning that their false accusation of his guilt will not pass unnoticed or unrequited in the end points to the cruel error that arises from their too rigidly maintained theology.

20   Zophar describes what awaits the wicked

20.2–3   The further we proceed with the dialogue the more repetitious become the speeches of the friends. Zophar begins by expressing his sense of outrage at Job's arguments. He is compelled to reply by an irresistible force. What is meant by *a spirit beyond my understanding* is not immediately obvious. Perhaps REB intends Zophar to claim divine revelation for what he is about to say.

20.4–11   The rest of his harangue is a description of the fate which awaits the wicked, decked out in many different figures of speech. This, he claims, is teaching which has been known since the beginning of human life on earth, and surely Job must know it. The prosperity and happiness of the evil man lasts a brief moment. However exalted he may be he is quickly swept away, and vanishes from society as completely as a dream. The punishment is passed on to his descendants. His sons will be forced to hand back the riches he gathered and will become so destitute that they will plead for relief from the poor. He himself will die young in full vigour.[1]

20.12–22   With v. 12 Zophar reverts to the wicked man in his lifetime. In a number of coarse images he says that he will be compelled to vomit out his evil plans and wicked deeds. Ill-gotten gains will have to be repaid. God will himself administer the emetic to the man who oppressed the poor, seized houses that he did not build, and was

[1] Note that REB reverses vv. 10 and 11 to place the reference to the sons after the wicked man's death. There seems no need to do this. As has been pointed out, our poet is not writing an essay.

ruthless in his greed. The punishment will come just as he has satisfied every need.

20.23–28   At the end of his speech Zophar emphasizes that it is God who sends all these punishments (though this is merely hinted at in the verbs of the Hebrew – REB has added *God* in v. 23). The attack with arrows recalls Job's bitter picture of God's onslaughts upon him (6.4; 7.18–220; 10.17). In the end fire and flood will destroy his home.

20.29   The final verse, as often in these speeches, summarizes what has been argued: this is the divine retribution that awaits the wicked.

As he listens to Job Zophar becomes more and more angry because he seems to be cutting at the root of God's just rule of the universe. If the wicked are not punished he feels that the moral order will collapse. Here is the cause of his fierce assertions. Whether they apply to Job no longer matters. This is the faith on which he was brought up. To question this is to put an axe at the root of his whole religion. It is Zophar's last word. He will not speak again.

21   Job flatly denies Zophar's argument

Zophar had argued that God always punished the wicked. This Job now flatly denies, and in this chapter he asks how often have the friends actually seen disaster strike an evil man.

21.2–6   The friends came to console Job, but their words have only increased his pain. It will be sufficient for him if they will simply listen to what he has to say. This will bring him comfort. They need be in no hurry to reply, for his complaint is against God, not against human beings. Let them just pay heed to his special case and sense its horror.

21.7–22   Zophar had said the wicked die young (20.5, 11): Job alleges that they live to a good old age, powerful and with their full vigour. Bildad claimed that the evil man leaves no children to follow him (18.19): Job says that their children are *settled around them* and their descendants flourish. Eliphaz had spoken of the destruction of the homes of the wicked (15.20), Bildad described the fire that burnt their tent (18.15), and Zophar affirmed that the wellbeing of evil men was transient (20.5, 21): Job claims that the reverse is the case – *their households* are *secure and safe*, their cattle breed without mishap, they are surrounded by a multitude of children, and *live out their days in prosperity*. At the end they *go down to Sheol in peace*, in the same way that Eliphaz had described the end of the righteous man (5.24–26). Yet these are men who have repudiated God and refuse to obey him. They seem fully in control of their destiny. Bildad had presented the image of the lamp of the wicked being snuffed out (18.6): how often does this actually happen? says Job. The psalmist had sung of the destruction of the wicked, blown away like chaff in the wind (Ps. 1.4): again Job questions whether it happens very frequently. The friends had tried to defend the doctrine of exact retribution by alleging that the punishment due to the evil man sometimes fell upon his children – it is traditional teaching (cf. Exod. 20.5, see Eliphaz, 5.4, and Zophar, 20.10, although there the suffering inflicted on the sinner's children is an additional punishment to his own): Job says that such a transfer of punishment is unjust. The individual should pay in full for his iniquities. Verse 22 can be fitted into the speech only with difficulty. Some scholars have deleted it as a gloss; others think Job is expressing an objection by the friends. Those who defend it explain it as meaning that Job is blaming the friends for foisting their own unyielding dogma upon God, who does not need them to teach him how to rule the world. Whatever the exact sense may be, it is clear that Job is unwilling to make any excuse for God. He is creator and ruler, and he must take responsibility for the inequalities in the world.

21.23–26 So far Job has concentrated on the prosperity of the wicked, which he claims he can substantiate from his own experience. Now he denies that there is any justice in human affairs for all are equal in death. One man comes to the end of his life *crowned with success*, enjoying *security and comfort*, and with rude good health. Another man has *never tasted prosperity*. They are laid side by side in the grave and *worms are the shroud of both*. It is a scepticism akin to that of Qoheleth (Ecclesiastes) (Eccl. 2.14; 3.19; 9.2, cf. Ps. 49.10).

21.27–33 To back up his own experience Job calls in the reports of travellers, who will have had a wide knowledge of the world. They will corroborate all that he has been claiming. The *wicked person is spared when disaster comes*. So secure is such a one that no one will dare to rebuke him for his evil deeds. And when he dies crowds flock to show their respect at his funeral.

21.34 This is how Job sees the world. It is no wonder that his speech ends with a reproach. *How futile is the comfort* they have tried to bring him through their speeches! *How false your answers ring!*

Job and the friends have now come into direct conflict. Both believe that their description of the world and of God's rule fits the facts. For the friends, however, this is largely dogma, learnt from the wise men who came before them, although Eliphaz in particular backs it up with revelation and experience, and all would aver that what can actually be seen in the world supports their theology. For Job it is a matter of immediate personal concern, not just because he is the innocent sufferer who disproves their theories but because his innocence is of vital concern to him and his need to meet with God is urgent and compelling.

22 *Eliphaz asserts Job's guilt*

In his third speech Eliphaz allows the logic of his theology to override all concern for Job and the evidence of his goodness. Since Job is being punished so severely he must be a great sinner, and his only hope is to repent.

22.2–5 Eliphaz first affirms God's impartiality. No one can bring him any benefit. It can be of no *advantage* to him if Job were *righteous* and he would gain nothing from Job's *perfection* (the adjective derived from this verb is translated 'blameless' in 1.8 and the theme is important in the book). God is not punishing Job for his *piety*. It is his great sin which has brought this great punishment upon him.

22.6–11 Then, with horrifying confidence, Eliphaz proceeds to list the sins of which Job must be guilty. He has taken pledges and left the poor without covering. The law required that if a poor man's outer garment was taken as a pledge for a loan it should be handed back at night because it was the only blanket that he possessed (Exod. 22.26–27; Deut. 24.12–13). Eliphaz accuses Job of such callous ruthlessness that the poor have left naked. He has withheld food and water from those in desperate need. This was not specified in the law, but the prophet whose words are preserved at the end of the book of Isaiah said that the true fast which God desired was 'sharing your food with the hungry' (Isa. 58.7), and Ezekiel describes the righteous man as the one who 'oppresses no one, . . . returns the debtor's pledge, . . . gives his food to the hungry and clothes those who have none' (Ezek. 18.7). He has *sent widows away empty-handed* and given no help to the *fatherless*. Care for those who have no one to stand up for them is a prominent feature of the Old Testament ethic (see Exod. 22.22–23; Deut. 24.17; 27.19; Isa. 1.17, 23; 10.1–2; Ezek. 22.7; Zech. 7.10). Eliphaz finds in such wrongs which Job must have committed the obvious cause of his suffering. Bildad has depicted the snares which lay in the path of a wicked man and the terrors which haunted him (18.5–12) and in his second speech Eliphaz had set out the fears with which evil men were continually racked (15.20–21). Now he says that since Job is such a sinner it is no wonder that he is filled with *sudden terror*. Verse 8 breaks the direct address to Job and some wish to remove it. Perhaps it is an oblique reference to Job, accusing him of being an oppressor.

22.12–20   Eliphaz goes further in his indictment of Job. He suggests that Job, like all evildoers, believes that God is too distant to pay any attention to his actions. That God dwells above the heights of the heaven led two psalmists to conclude that he could see everything that human beings did (Pss. 14.2; 33.13f.), while another claimed that the wicked reckoned that he was too far off to have any interest in their doings (73.11, cf. Isa. 29.15). This is not so, says Eliphaz, and he urges Job to consider how God's punishment falls upon those who commit evil: *their riches are swept away* and they themselves are *snatched off before their time*. Verses 17–18 recall 21.14–16. Eliphaz reminds Job of what he has said, only to follow with a complete reversal of Job's assertion that it is rare for such persons to be punished (cf. 21.17–18).

22.21–30   Since Job is plainly marked out by God as a sinner, Eliphaz concludes by appealing to him to turn back to God and *accept* his *instruction*. If he repents and puts away his wrongdoing God will restore his prosperity. It is surprising that Eliphaz should say that if Job renounces his wealth he will find that God is his true treasure (vv. 24–25). Has he forgotten that Job has lost all he ever had? In any case this conflicts with his theology, which links goodness and prosperity indivisibly together, rather than finding in fellowship with God a prize greater than any treasure of precious metals. If he glimpses this higher way, it is for a brief moment. He soon returns to his description of the righteous man, successful in all his dealings, and he ends his speech by contrasting God's protection of the *humble* and *innocent* with his abasing of the *haughty*.

It seems incredible that the kindliest of the three friends should have been so certain of his theology that he can hurl such accusations at Job. He is convinced, however, that piety and prosperity belong together. It easily leads to a piety which is adopted in order to secure the prosperity. Eliphaz is unable to comprehend Job's greater piety which holds on to his innnocence and to the God whose actions are inexplicable to him. The prosperity is essential for Eliphaz. While Job's theology is the same as that of the friends, he nowhere regrets his integrity and will not deny it in the hope of a return to God's favour.

23–24   *Job's answer to Eliphaz*

With this speech we run into considerable difficulties and it is convenient to discuss the rest of the third cycle of speeches with this chapter.

The problem is this. In the third cycle there is no speech by Zophar and only an extremely short speech by Bildad. By itself this could readily be explained as indicating that the friends ran out of arguments. Coupled with the lack of a complete set of speeches, however, is the fact that in these chapters Job often speaks like the friends rather than uttering his usual criticisms and doubts, and this has suggested to many scholars that something is wrong with the text. Perhaps the poet did not complete the third cycle, and we are left with fragments that he intended to work up into a full debate. Others explain the inconsistencies in Job's words by proposing that he is quoting at length from the friends (Hebrew does not possess quotation marks, although in narrative there is seldom any difficulty in following what the actors say because there are indications of change of speaker). Others again transfer part of Job's speeches to Bildad and Zophar, although there is insufficient material to complete a full cycle. For this reason it has been proposed that an editor removed what he found quite outrageous in Job's utterances and substituted more orthodox statements in less impressive poetry.

In this commentary we shall first draw out the meaning of the words as they stand, before considering whether the text has suffered any damage.

23.2–5   Job begins by expressing his bitterness at the way God has pressed harshly upon him. Yet because he is confident of his own innocence and still holds on to the traditional theology of a just recompense for a man's deeds, he has a deep longing to present his case before God. If only he could get through to God he feels confident that he could convince him that he is blameless and that there has been some ghastly mistake in the misfortunes which have been hurled upon him. So he repeats the urgent pleas that he had uttered in 9.34f. and 13.21–22. As then, he declares that he is ready either to set out his own defence or to reply to God's accusations.

23.6–7   Unlike his earlier mood, he now denies that God would simply *browbeat* him by using his irresistible power (contrast 9.3, 14–20, 22f., 34f.; 13.31 with 23.6). Despite all appearances he trusts in the integrity of the divine court where *the upright are vindicated* and he will win *an outright acquittal* from his judge.

23.8–9   But he cannot find God. On an earlier occasion Job had said that even when God moved past him he was unaware of his presence (9.11). Now God eludes his persistent search. Points of the compass were defined in ancient Israel by facing east, so that the north is the left hand and the south the right. As the alternative translations in the margin show, Job may be moving forward and backward, and turning to the left and right.

23.10–12   Even though he cannot reach God he retains his confidence that God knows all that he does. So certain is he of his innocence that he boldly affirms that he can face any testing, confident that he will emerge unscathed. Christians have been so conditioned to unmask hypocrisy that we may easily mistake Job's disposition in these verses. Crushed by his suffering which the friends interpret at evidence of his guilt, and holding the same basic belief in the connection between sin and punishment, the wonder is that he withstands the pressure of the friends and the silence of his God and still refuses to deny what he knows to be true. He has kept God's path. He has obeyed God's commands. He has *treasured* in his *heart* all that God says. Only by holding on to this can he maintain his integrity.

23.13–17   Yet how difficult it is! God is all-powerful. He will carry out his purposes. No one can deflect him. That is why Job is still *fearful*. He longs to meet God in order to set the record straight, yet he knows what kind of a God it is that he will meet. *Mystery* hides God, but in spite of his incomprehensible awesomeness, he will still approach him.

This majestic and all-powerful God will open the grand assize – but when this will be no one knows. Once again reverence and doubt intermingle in Job's mind. This is the Job we have met already many times. And at the end of the chapter Job utters a defiant challenge to anyone to dispute what he has set forth. The question is, what did Job present?

24.2, 6, 3, 9, 4   As can be seen from the verse numbers and the margin, REB rearranges vv. 3–9 'to restore the natural order'. What the natural order is, however, depends upon how the vignettes of various evil-doers and the poor are interpreted. Following the pattern of this commentary we shall accept the interpretation of REB, and leave it to other commentators to provide alternatives.

The first five verses describe those who pay little heed to the law. They enlarge their holdings by moving *boundary stones* and *pasture flocks* which *they have stolen* there (cf. Deut. 19.14; 27.17; Hos. 5.10; Prov. 20.28; 23.10). They take crops that do not belong to them and pilfer the *late grapes*.[1] Instead of caring for the fatherless and the widow they steal their donkeys and oxen. They take a child at the breast as a pledge for a loan and deal ruthlessly with the poor.

24.5, 7–8, 10–12   The next account is of those who are utterly destitute. Starving, they have to search the barren steppe for food. Those who are day labourers receive such low wages that their children *go hungry*. The plight of those with no covering against the cold, cowering against the rocks to find what little shelter they can against the rain forms the next vivid word picture. These impoverished day labourers *carry the sheaves* but have no bread to eat themselves, tread out the grapes but have no share in the wine. Without any security in the city, they cry out to God, but he *remains deaf to their prayer*. Here the authentic Job surely is speaking. God fails to answer the cry of the sufferers, as he is silent to his own pleading.

24.14–17   There follow wrongdoers who commit their crimes under the cloak of darkness: the murderer who seems to kill just for the thrill of killing; the *seducer* who creeps into a woman's house at

[1] Why these thieves should take them from the *rich man's vineyard* is not clear. In the surrounding verses the law-breakers appear to be the rich and powerful, whereas here the crime is that committed by the poor.

nightfall; the burglar who *prowls about* in disguise and in the dark digs through the mud wall of a house that he has *marked down during the day*. These all carry out their nefarious practices at a time when honest citizens fear to venture out. Darkness is as day to them. No comment follows, and what significance Job places upon these descriptions is uncertain. Possibly he is pointing out that these wrongdoers operate in the dark when their fellow human beings do not see them – and God seems not to see them either. But if the section is linked with the closing verses of the chapter, as REB sets it out, the writer is saying the reverse of this. Although these deeds are performed in the night God *is* aware and will punish all those who commit such crimes.

24.18–25 For REB continues without a break. A curse lies on their fields. No one will work for them. They are carried off to death as swiftly as the snow melts under the hot sun. God brings them to judgment. Suddenly his stroke falls and they are no more. The friends would fully concur with this account of the swift and unexpected death of the wicked, and it is difficult to see what point there could be in Job's question, *If this is not so, who will prove me wrong?*

25   Bildad's final word

In reply to Job's question Bildad can muster no more than five verses! It seems unlikely, however, that this is what our poet intended. The speech seems to have lost its beginning. All the other speeches make some reference to what has gone before. Bildad opens with a description of God, and even this is suspect for the pronoun *him* lacks an antecedent.

What remains are allusions to God's power and his purity, in the face of which no *mere mortal* can be *justified* or *regarded as virtuous*. Even the moon and stars are impure in his sight. How then can human beings be found undefiled, who are so insignificant as to be no more than maggots?

So far the text goes and no further. We leave a discussion of whether any part of Bildad's speech can be recovered until we have considered Job's words in chs. 26–27.

26–27   *A tangle of speeches*

Job's final speech makes it difficult to avoid the conclusion that the text is in disarray. It extends for six chapters, by far the longest speech matched only by those of Elihu; ch. 28 is a self-contained poem; there is a fresh introduction in 27.1, and this is in an unusual form; chs. 29–31 form a concluding soliloquy and appeal by Job in themselves and match ch. 3; and much of what Job says in chs. 26–27 echoes the teaching of the friends rather than the attitudes which he has expressed earlier.

Each of these peculiarities can be accounted for to some extent, but cumulatively they form a strong case for maintaining that the third cycle of speeches as we have it is not the final intention of our poet. We have already noted that inconsistent teaching has been explained as quotations or sarcasm. Some have proposed that there was a pause after the end of ch. 26 while Job waits for Zophar to speak. It was when he failed to do so that Job *resumed his discourse*, replying to the friends in ch. 27 and making his final challenge in chs. 29–31. Chapter 28 stands so much apart that even if it is not taken to be an interpolation by a later editor it is rarely ascribed to Job. Perhaps the poet himself speaks, or he envisages a bystander making a contribution which has the dramatic effect of holding back the denouement of the action and gives the reader time to think over what has been said so far. REB simply translates the text, making only the comment that ch. 28 describes 'God's unfathomable wisdom' and chs. 29–31 are 'Job's final survey of his case'. We shall proceed as before by initially expounding the text as it lies before us.

26.2–4   Job begins by rounding on Bildad for his failure to give him any support. He is *powerless* and *bereft of wisdom*, but Bildad's words are inappropriate to his need. The address is singular, unlike Job's normal way of speaking to the three friends together (the only exceptions are 16.3; 12.7f.; 21.3), but too much should not be made of this.

26.5–14   The remainder of the chapter consists of a description of the power of God. Some ascribe it to Bildad, noting that it continues his account of God's omnipotence. On the other hand Job is very conscious of God's might, and flinches before it, fearful that even if he managed to reach him and present his case God would simply crush him by his superior strength (9.15–20, 32–35; 13.20–21). Moreover he has referred to God's triumph over the *sea monster* and *Rahab* before (7.12; 9.8, 13). There is no intrinsic impossibility in accepting these verses as by Job, the only difficulty is that they are not closely related to his main argument but read as the description by an interested observer who is not intimately involved in the way God rules the world. It seems unlikely, therefore, that our poet intended them originally as part of Job's speech, or if he did, that they have been fully integrated into such a speech. To ascribe them to Bildad is entirely arbitrary, however.

God's power is seen to reach to the underworld. The *shades* are the dead who live out a gloomy existence in Sheol, the land of 'destruction' (the basic meaning of *Abaddon*), situated under the waters beneath the earth. As our poet displays God's might through the universe he has created we are given a clear picture of the way the ancients viewed the world. The *earth* is suspended *over the void* with the sky a solid dome over it, suspended on *pillars* which are shaken by the *thunder of his voice*. The waters are held in the *clouds*, imagined as huge water-skins. The 'circle of the waters', the *horizon*, is *the boundary between light and darkness*. Ancient stories are recalled to expand upon God's greatness. From Ugarit come accounts of the battles between Baal and Yam (REB points to the reminiscence by its translation *sea monster*. Elsewhere in the Old Testament there are allusions to God's defeat of those other monsters *Rahab* (Ps. 40.4; 82.4; 83.10; Isa. 30.7; 51.9), and the *twisting sea serpent* (Isa. 27.1), both also present in the mythology from the ancient Middle East. In a wonderfully evocative phrase, such massive greatness as we can descry is *but the fringes of his power*; we hear but a *faint whisper* of him. Far vaster and more incomprehensible must be his full omnipotence.

27.2–6   The resumed discourse begins with words that belong to the authentic Job. He swears an oath that he will utter no untruth. To abandon his conviction of his innocence would be to deny the very ground upon which his own integrity and the righteousness of the universe are established, and so long as he lives he will never abandon this conviction. The passage is striking. Job swears by the life of God himself that he will maintain his integrity, yet in that very breath declares that this God has denied him justice. The God to whom he appeals and the God against whom he appeals lie side by side.

27.7–10   Suddenly all is changed. The evildoer is suddenly struck down by God. He will have no hope when God *takes away his life*. God will not hear his prayer, and it will be useless for him to cry out to God when disaster comes, since he has neglected him at other times. The wish that one's *enemy* might suffer the fate of such sinner grates on our sensibilities, but is similar to much that is found in the psalms (see e.g. Pss. 69.22–28; 109.1–20). This is not at all what Job has argued earlier. His complaint has been that the wicked enjoy a long life of prosperity (21.7–21) and that no difference can be discerned between the fate of the pious and the ungodly (21.23–26). It is the friends who claim that goodness and prosperity are linked while the evil man faces divine punishment.

27.11–12 The address in vv. 11–12 is in the plural, and partly because of this, partly because it does not conflict with Job's overall position, it may be that here is another fragment of one of his speeches. If by Job, the meaning would be that he is only proclaiming what God actually does and that God's actions are immediately obvious to everyone who will look carefully at the affairs of men. The arguments of the friends are *empty nonsense*, and do not accord with the facts of life.

27.13–23 The remainder of the chapter reverts to the traditional orthodoxy and sets out the punishments which God sends upon the wicked. His sons will *fall by the sword*. Any who survive will starve and die from disease, leaving no widows to *weep for them*. Although they amass great wealth, the righteous will inherit it. Their homes will be as fragile as a *bird's nest* or the temporary *shelter* of poles and branches or reeds put up at harvest time by those watching the ripening crops. Their riches will be snatched away in a moment, during a single night. REB finds a single simile in vv. 20–23: disaster will overtake them like a storm, with winds that mock their frailty.

It is possible that part of this was intended as Zophar's missing speech, but we do not know, and all that can be said is that several sections of these two chapters accord ill with Job's earlier protests. It cannot be that the friends have convinced him that their reading of the world is right.

28 *God's unfathomable wisdom*

This is clearly an independent poem on wisdom, artfully constructed in three sections with a refrain in vv. 12 and 20. Some believe that the refrain originally also opened the poem, but there is no trace of this in the manuscript evidence, and the refrain is found in slightly different forms at its two appearances which may go against the suggestion.

What is this wisdom? The wise men had often personified wisdom, most notably the writer of the first nine chapters of Proverbs, where wisdom is present at the very creation of the world, 'the first of [God's] works', when 'there was yet no ocean' and 'before the mountains were settled in their place' (Prov. 8.22–31). Elsewhere wisdom is seen as a teacher (Prov. 1.20–33; 8.1–11, 32–36). The noun happens to be feminine in gender in Hebrew, and although we need to be careful not to confuse gender with sex, it was easy to depict wisdom as a woman who offers her favours to the young men (Prov. 9.1–6). In the intertestamental Ben Sira (Ecclesiasticus) there is increasing use of sexual imagery (Ecclus. 14.22–25; 51.13–21), but the ideas of wisdom as a teacher (Ecclus. 4.11–19; 51.13–30) and as cosmic wisdom continue (Ecclus. 1.1–10; 24.1–22). A striking development in Ben Sira, however, is the identification of wisdom with the Jewish Law (Ecclus. 15.1; 24.8–12, 23–29), domesticating wisdom which otherwise might have become a consort to Yahweh, or even a rival. In the present chapter wisdom is no more than a personification of the mysterious 'laws' which control the universe.

28.1–11   The first stanza contains lively sketches of mining activities. The miners work in darkness, at the end of long passages. Foreign slaves are the main labourers in this dangerous work. Our poet depicts them hanging on the end of swaying ropes, *forgotten* by those whose lives are spent above ground. He contrasts the corn-fields on the surface and the mining operations below, where the spoil is raked over like a fire. *Lapis lazuli* was highly valued by the ancients, and specks of yellow iron pyrites in it gleam like gold. Into this strange and obscure world the birds of prey, noted for their keen sight, are unable to look, and the greatest of the animals is excluded. It is man's ingenuity which *cuts galleries in the rocks* and *lays bare* the foundations of the *mountains*, which *dams up* the streams so that the mine is not flooded, and brings out *hidden riches* from under the earth.

28.12–27   Yet for all his technical skill man does not know the road to *wisdom*. That path is concealed from everyone. The primeval *ocean* declares it is not in its depths. It cannot be purchased with the costliest of gems. No earthly creature or bird flying in the skies has seen it. Even *destruction* (retained as 'Abaddon' in 26.6), the land of the dead and death *know of it only by hearsay*. God alone *understands the way to* wisdom, for he is the maker of the universe and controls all its forces.

28.28   The final verse has often been held to be a later addition, but there seems no reason to question it. If it is removed the poem ends in ignorance. God alone knows and understands wisdom. The verse, however, accepts this, and then points out to human beings what is wisdom for them: reverence toward God and abandoning evil.

It has sometimes been suggested that two different conceptions of wisdom are found in this chapter. The wisdom which God knows is cosmic, the secrets of the universe. This wisdom is for ever out of the reach of mankind. For men and women, however, there remains moral wisdom, which is their true blessing. Whether it is right to distinguish between the two aspects of wisdom is uncertain. After all it is the same word which is used for both.

Some regard this poem as totally irrelevant to the debate. It is complete in itself. It is lyrical, not argumentative. It foreshadows the divine speeches and weakens their impact. In the mouth of Job is it out of place. But why should it not have been intended as spoken by an anonymous bystander? It marks the end of the ever more fractious dispute. It gives Job time to withdraw from the argument and look back over his life. When he speaks again he will be calmer, but no less confident of his integrity.

29–31   *Job's final survey of his case*

With careful attention to the structure of his work our poet matches Job's first speech with this final soliloquy. The text is difficult in several places and sometimes the thought strikes the modern reader as rather incoherent. REB adopts various emendations and new meanings of words, and makes a number of transpositions. As is our policy in this commentary we shall accept REB as it stands.

The three chapters mark the divisions in the speech. In ch. 29 Job looks back to his happy life before the disasters struck. He was an honoured elder statesman in the city, and everyone deferred to him. On his part he looked after those who had no one to protect them. He then turns to the present in ch. 30 and describes the woeful state to which he has fallen. Even the lowest members of society scoff at him and God has become his enemy. Finally he affirms his innocence in a great oath of clearance, ending with an urgent request to meet God to hear his indictment and present his case.

The three friends are forgotten and Job is alone before his God. One can appreciate the suggestion that an early stage in the development of the book of Job consisted of the folk-story and these three chapters, together with ch. 3, but there is no way of telling whether our poet first wrote a narrative poem without dialogue, in which Job was the only speaker. It is equally possible to see these chapters as the frame within which the debate with the friends is set, and to accept that this was our poet's original plan for his book.

29.2–10, 21–25   The introduction to ch. 29 is the same as that in 27.1, but here it would mark a resumption after the poem about wisdom. In the *old days* God watched over Job in a benign way, very different from the spying of which Job had accused him in 10.14; 13.27; 14.16. It is the loving protection which is part of the priestly blessing in Num. 6.24 and of which the psalmist sings (Ps. 121.7f.). In those days which now appear to be so distant God had indeed 'hedged him round with his protection' and Job rejoiced in it. His farms prospered. When he went to take his seat in the *gate*, the only open space in a city tightly packed with houses and narrow alleys, and the natural place for the leaders of the community to meet and discuss affairs or settle disputes, young men *kept back out of sight* and even the elders held him in the highest respect. REB moves vv. 21–25 to follow v. 10 and so keeps together the description of Job's position among the city leaders. The other men of the city listened to his words in silence, and his counsel was as eagerly looked for as the spring rains which were essential for the maturing of the crops. Picking up a military metaphor, Job presents himself as a king with authority over his army. *Like one who comforts mourners* fits in very badly on this interpretation. It might be seen as a transition to the next part of the speech, but even so it is odd to find it linked with the metaphor of an army commander in an account of the way Job *presided over* the council. Some see it as a hint that the friends have not given him a similar comfort, but this does not relieve the sudden change of image.

29.11–17   The respect in which Job is held does not lie in his wealth or power but in his integrity and concern for those without anyone to stand up for them. He *saved the poor who appealed for help*, he defended the *fatherless*, and *widows* were made happy because he supported them. In simple and telling phrases Job speaks of the way he was *eyes to the blind, feet to the lame*, and *a father to the needy*. Those who did not have a secure place in the local society were likely to be taken advantage of, and Job says he *took up* their *cause*. In language not to be taken literally he *broke the fangs of the miscreant* and rescued those who had been attacked.

29.18–20   Job's theology was that of the friends. Such goodness would assuredly receive divine blessing, so he expected to reach a ripe old age with his *powers unimpaired*. Like the psalmist he pictured himself as a tree with water continually at its roots (Ps. 1.3). The image changes to a bow, the symbol of strength (cf. Gen. 49.24; the breaking of the bow meant the destruction of a nation's military power: Ps. 46.9; Jer. 49.35; Hos. 1.5). And here, if we follow REB's transposition of vv. 21–25, Job's review of his time of happiness ends.

30.1–8   As he turns to his present sufferings we detect a new bitterness. He is mocked by the young outcasts of society, and this brings him to describe those who scoff at him in words that show little sympathy for their plight. He declares that he would not have put their fathers on a level with his watch dogs. To feel the force of Job's comment it is necessary to remember that the Israelites, and the people of the Middle East generally, were not dog lovers, and dogs were seen as no more than scavengers and became a term of contempt (cf. I Sam. 17.43; II Sam. 3.8; 16.9; I Kings 14.11; 21.19, 23; Ps. 68.23). Such poor wretches had to try to survive on *roots* and desert plants. They were hounded out of the villages as if they were *thieves*, and the only shelter they could find was in the bare mountain *gullies*. Their howling is probably due to hunger and cold.

30.15–19   The only excuse for showing such contempt for such wretched outcasts is that Job has sunk so low that even the most despised rejects of society now feel able to taunt him. They *shun* him and *spit* in his face. Like a besieging army which has breached the walls of a city, they remorselessly attack him.

It is small wonder that he is overwhelmed with *terror*. All *hope of deliverance* has *vanished*. His days are filled with *misery* and at night *pain pierces* his *bones*. The picture in v. 18 is of a sick man choking in his own *phlegm*, but since Eastern garments do not have tight-fitting collars, the exact simile is difficult to determine. *God* has been added in the next verse to indicate who the subject of the verb is. Without naming him, Job blames God for his misfortunes.

30.20–23 As so often, while the friends can speak of God with cool detachment, the mere thought makes Job turn to God in prayer. But God is still the silent one who will not answer his call, the distant one who keeps *aloof*. He is the cruel oppressor who *persecutes* and will *hand* him *over to death* after he has finished his torture.

30.24–31 Job cannot abandon his belief that goodness should be rewarded. He returns to the charity he used to give to beggars, gifts which were not given to ease his conscience but which came from a heart which was grieved at their sufferings. Yet *evil* came where he *expected good*. The *ferment* in his *bowels* may be a description of his illness, but the bowels are the seat of the emotions in Israelite psychology, and the meaning may be that he is in anguish because of his plight. So he returns to the account of his physical distress, with only the wild animals for his companions (unless the meaning is that his cries for help are like theirs). His skin turns black and *peels off*. He has no shade from the scorching *heat*. The joyful music of his earlier life has turned into *weeping* and *a dirge*.

At the beginning of ch. 31 says that he has *taken an oath never to let his eyes linger on a girl*. Far from committing adultery, he has refrained from a lustful glance. Because vv. 2–4 do not follow naturally after this, REB has moved the verses to follow v. 5. Such transpositions are arbitrary and may not accord with Eastern sensitivity, although this and the other changes later in the chapter suit our Western ideas of logical development.

31.2–4 As REB presents the speech, Job begins his declaration of innocence by repeating his sense of outrage that God, who should maintain justice by punishing wrongdoers, appears indifferent to his piety and purity.

31.5–6 He then opens his oath of clearance. May punishment fall upon him if he has committed any of these crimes. He has kept apart from *falsehood* and *deceit*, here personified. He has avoided any lustful glance on any woman.[1] If God would *weigh* him *in the scales of justice* he would know that he is *blameless* (the word is the one used by God to describe Job in 2.3, and thrown at Job by his wife in 2.9). Our poet is a master of irony.

---

[1] The Hebrew has 'virgin' as more to be desired. The REB *girl*, which feminists today object to as being sexist, perhaps reproduces the overtones of the word in the patriarchal age.

31.7–8 Picking up his oath, Job affirms that he has not *wandered from the way* of uprightness to covet what belongs to another (if that is the meaning of *if my heart has followed my eyes*), and the coveting is probably wider than a desire for the wife of another man, although the divisions of the text in REB perhaps imply that the translators took the whole section vv. 5–8 as referring to sexual desire, followed by a rejection of adultery in vv. 9–12. Having clean hands is often a symbol of righteousness (17.9; 22–30; Pss. 18.20, 24; 24.4, cf. Ps. 26.6). Here Job denies that any *dirt has stuck to his hands*. The punishment which the oath invokes follows: may his crops be seized or destroyed.

31.9–12 Our poet has already sketched the adulterer waiting eagerly for twilight (24.15). Here Job repudiates this sin in an oath which we today find repellent. If he has found a neighbour's wife attractive and has *lurked* at his door to find an opportunity of lying with her, he swears that his wife may *be another man's slave* (the Hebrew is more vivid, 'may she grind corn for someone else') and other men may have sexual intercourse with her. Adultery, Job affirms, is a *heinous act*, an offence which can be brought before the judges. It is like a fire that rages through the ripe corn.[2] It has to be remembered that in ancient Israel adultery was an offence against the husband. The punishment which Job envisages is the strict retribution of the *talion* (eye for eye and tooth for tooth); if he committed adultery, his own sexual rights over his own wife may be violated.

31.13–15 More atttractive to our ways of thinking is the next set of practices which Job says have formed the pattern of his life. If the law was properly observed, slaves in Israel had a better time than in some of the other countries of the ancient Middle East (cf. Exod. 21.2–11; Deut. 15.12–18; cf. Lev. 25.39–46), and we should not compare slavery there with that on the plantations in America and the Caribbean islands. Nevertheless, the life of slaves was hard and they were at the mercy of their masters. Job says that he recognized that slaves were human beings, created by God as he was, and that he listened to their complaint. He acknowledges that he is responsible to God for his treatment of his slaves.

31.16–23 The poor, widows, and the fatherless were those members of society without protection and with no one to secure their rights. Job says that he has met the need of the poor, has never caused

---

[2] The word represented by *destructive* is 'Abaddon' (cf. 26.6; 28.22).

distress to widows, has shared his food with the fatherless, and has provided clothing for all those in want. Although his wealth and position gave him great power he never used his influence to exploit those who were defenceless. His reverence for God constrained him to care for all these vulnerable and impoverished groups. Verse 18 is taken to mean that Job had 'adopted' some orphans.[3]

31.24–28   Verses 24–28 combine the idolatry of trusting in riches rather than in God, and the idolatry of worshipping the sun and moon. Kissing the hand in homage is probably to be seen as throwing kisses to the moon. Worship of the heavenly beings occurred from time to time in Israel (cf. II Kings 21.3–5; 23.4), and is frequently condemned (Deut. 4.19; 17.2–4; Jer. 8.1f.).

31.38–40   At this point REB inserts vv. 38–40. Certainly they form an odd conclusion to the chapter and destroy the effect of the climax of Job's appeal to God in vv. 35–37. The main problem about moving verses in this way is that it is difficult to see how they came to be displaced, and it may be that our poet had different stylistic criteria from ours. However, we shall still follow the REB.

The reason why Job's land may have *cried out in reproach* is that he has purloined its *produce*. As the margin indicates, the sense of the word translated *creditors* (mg. *tenants*) is not clear. Perhaps the crime that is envisaged is of securing the death of the rightful owner and appropriating his fields, rather like Ahab with Naboth's vineyard (I Kings 21). The REB text seems to mean that Job has rented fields and not paid what was due at the time of harvest. The margin presumably treats the two halves of the verse independently, and finds in the second line some form of oppression of those who rent their fields from him. Again it is a 'poetic justice' punishment. The fields that have been wronged will fail to produce good crops. Instead weeds will be all that will grow.

31.29–30   Job tells of his treatment of his enemies. To curse them would certainly be wrong, but he goes further and denies ever being glad when disaster befell them.

31.31–32   He then returns to his treatment of the needy. His servants and slaves will testify that he has shared his food with them. More, he has always been ready to receive a benighted traveller into his

---

[3] Strictly *fatherless* is correct, since it was the loss of the *father* which removed both the breadwinner and the protector of the 'orphan'.

home. We may recall Lot's welcome of the two angels (Gen. 19.1–2) and contrast the refusal of the men of Gibeah to give a night's lodging to the Levite who was returning from Bethlehem-Judah with the ready offer of lodging by the old man (Judg. 19.15–21).

31.34–37 Finally he denies that he has committed any secret sins, wrongs concealed from his fellow townsmen – and breaks off to appeal directly to God. If the *witness* is human this line may go with what comes before and be a further reinforcement of his declaration of complete innocence. More probably, however, it is God himself (or just possibly the mediator who has appeared on several occasions before). More directly Job demands that God should specify the charges which he is bringing against him. By transposing a line from v. 34 to the end of v. 35, REB makes Job say that if he received God's indictment he would not skulk away,[4] but would treat it as a commendation which he would be proud to wear on his *shoulder* or set as *a crown on* his *head*. So confident is Job of his innocence and his upright life that he utters a challenge to God. That is the record which he would *present in court as* his *defence*.

There are a number of things to be observed in these chapters. First, it is significant that, although our poet has created characters who are not Israelites, their ideas of what is right are closely akin to the requirements of the Israelite law, though Job moves beyond it. Parallels to looking after the welfare of slaves and welcoming travellers into one's home have already been noted. Job's rejection of coveting recalls the Ten Commandments (Exod. 20.17; Deut. 5.21). Teaching against adultery is frequently found in the wisdom writings as well as in the law, though usually the wise men warn the young man to avoid the artful enticements of the adulteress and prostitute, and it is perhaps worth noting that Job would place the blame for adultery squarely on his own shoulders (31.9; cf. Prov. 6.32; 7.5–27; Exod. 20.14; Lev. 18.20; Deut. 22.22). Care for the poor, widows and orphans has a prominent place in the Old Testament but is not limited to Israel (cf. Exod. 22.21–27; 23.3–11; Deut. 10.18–19; 14.28–29; 15.7–11; 24.14–22; Amos 2.6–8; 4.1; 8.4–6; Isa. 3.14–15; 10.2; Jer. 5.28; 22.16; Zech. 7.9–10). Proverbs urges kindliness towards the poor but sometimes regards them as feckless (e.g. 14.21, 31; 17.5; 15.25; 19.17;

---

[4] Is there a reminiscence of the way the first man and woman hid from God in the garden (Gen. 3.8)? Probably not, for allusions to the Genesis story are lacking in the rest of the Old Testament and Job's silence is different from the way the first pair hid from God. Still less is it likely if REB's transposition is not accepted.

21.13; 22.9, 22; 23.11, but contrast 10.4; 12.11; 13.18; 21.17; 28.19). In the ancient Middle East generally the king was expected to protect the poor. In one of the narratives from Ugarit Yassib complains that his father Keret has not judged the cause of the widow or banished those who oppress the poor, and has not fed orphans and widows. In Egypt the Eloquent Peasant compliments his judge Reusi, 'You are a father to the orphan, a husband to the widow, a brother to the divorced.' Hammurabi says that the gods have named him to cause justice to prevail in the land so that the strong may not oppress the weak. (Cf. Ps. 72.2–4, 12–14 for an example of the duty of the king in the Old Testament.) There is much that is common in the ethical ideas across the ancient world, although perhaps the unprivileged have a greater place in the concern of the Old Testament.

Secondly, Job's plea of innocence appears to be a refutation of the charges which Eliphaz brought against him. With 29.11–17 and 31.16–23 compare 22.6–9, and alongside 31.24–25 set 22.24–25. Eliphaz had observed Job's misfortunes and suffering from which he inferred that he must be secret sinner (though many of the crimes he charged Job with are not such as could be hidden away). Job knows his own heart and actions, and refuses to bow either to the tirades of the friends or the apparent judgment of God.

Thirdly, we need still to keep in mind that Job has not abandoned the orthodox theology which he shares with the friends. He insists on presenting his case to God because he believes that there has been some ghastly miscarriage of justice. If only he could get through to God he could set matters right by proving that he was indeed innocent and did not deserve the sufferings inflicted upon him.

And finally we have to thrust from our minds all ideas of hypocrisy or the thought that Job could not possibly be as perfect as he claims to be. Our poet has gone to great lengths to emphasize that Job is indeed blameless, even though the friends question it. He states in his first verse that Job is 'a man of blameless and upright life, . . . who feared God and set his face against wrongdoing'. God twice affirms Job's goodness, using the same words (1.8; 2.3) and Job's wife recognizes Job's 'integrity', even though she says that it has done him little good (2.9). A group of words variously translated 'blameless' (1.1; 2.3; 8.20; 9.20, 21, 22; 12.4, 31.6), 'integrity' (2.3, 9), 'innocence' (27.5), 'perfect' (22.3) re-echo across the pages, alongside other terms such as 'upright' (1.1, 8; 2.3; 10.15), 'innocent' (12.4), 'righteous' (17.9), 'in the right' (9.15, 20), 'sincere' (16.7).

Job has made his final appeal. Will God respond? One onlooker does not appear to think so, for he jumps in with a series of long and repetitious speeches.

32–33   *The first speech of Elihu*

One has only to read this first speech by Elihu to see why many scholars think that our poet was not responsible for them. To our way of thinking Elihu is pompous, opinionated and verbose. He is introduced in six repetitious verses in which his anger is mentioned four times. He is not named in the opening narrative, and God does not mention him in the epilogue. He addresses Job by name in a way that none of the other friends do, and quotes from the earlier speeches, again unlike the previous practice. Whether the vocabulary is markedly different from the rest of the book is debated.

But we cannot know how the speeches struck the writer's first hearers. If Elihu is intended to look ridiculous, as appears to us, there seems no reason why our poet should not have presented such a character. If those hearers had different canons of style and sense of what is fitting, they may have accepted Elihu on his own estimation. It is impossible to tell. The writer of Ps. 119 can say that he has 'more insight that all [his] teachers' and 'more wisdom that those who are old' (Ps. 119.99–100), words which strike us as extremely boastful and brash, although the psalmist's spirit is very different from that of Elihu. If our poet wrote these chapters as well as the rest of the book, it seems likely that he intended Elihu as a caricature, otherwise there would be no point in the divine speeches and the concluding narrative, but we cannot be sure.

Perhaps it will be best to go through the speeches before we discuss the problem any further.

32.1–6   The beginning of the prose introduction refers to the friends strangely as 'three men', raising a further query about the originality of the Elihu speeches. Elihu is younger than the friends and is unable to restrain his anger because they have failed to answer Job and he thinks he could easily have performed this task. Alleging that Job had *made himself out to be more righteous than God*, he seems to mean either that Job had an overweening sense of his own goodness, or that he had set up his own standards of morality over against God's by his insistence on his own innocence and his accusations that God was not treating him justly. The alternative in the margin suggests that Elihu is angry because Job had succeeded so far in proving his innocence. That the friends had *found no answer to Job and so let God appear wrong* follows a Jewish tradition that this was the original text which was 'corrected' by the scribes (see mg.) because of its blasphemy. By abandoning the debate they had effectively allowed Job to win and thereby accepted that God was in the wrong.

32.7–10 Elihu emphasizes his youth. In accordance with normal custom he had waited for his elders to answer Job, expecting that the friends would possess wisdom, but now he has become convinced that God gives understanding to the young as well as to the old. Elihu shows a curious mixture of reticence and self-confidence, and by v. 10 is demanding a hearing.

32.11–14 With tedious repetitiveness Elihu says that he has carefully followed what the friends have said. None of them has succeeded in reproving Job or answering him. Verse 13 is oddly phrased but appears to say that the friends have admitted that Job is too clever for them and that only God can refute him. Elihu feels that there is no need for God to intervene. Unlike the friends he is able to produce a coherent case against Job.[1]

32.15–22 He can wait no longer, for he is bursting to express his opinions. Again with the self-confidence of youth he asserts that he will use no flattery but present his case with the complete impartiality which God requires. Surely, we feel, the writer of these lines intends to make Elihu appear absurd.

33.1–7 Elihu repeatedly demands attention to what he has to say. He has his answer ready. He is confident of his ability and wealth of knowledge. This very serious young man will certainly speak *with sincerity*. His wisdom comes from God. Yet he does not wish to *overawe* Job and points out that he is only human, so that he need not be afraid to answer him.

33.8–12 One of the features of the speeches by Elihu is the way he refers to earlier statements. Here he gives the gist of what Job has said on several occasions, quoting some of Job's words (cf. 9.21; 10.7; 12.4; 13.16–19; 16.17; 23.7, 10–12; 27.5–6; 29.14; 31 for Job's assertions

---

[1] As the mg. shows this is an emendation of the text. If the mg. is accepted Elihu says that Job has not yet had to face his more effective arguments.

of innocence, and 7.21; 10.13–17; 13.24–27; 14.16; 19.6–12 for his descriptions of God as his accuser and enemy).

33.13–22 To this Elihu makes a blunt denial: *You are not in the right*. In any case God is far greater than any human being and no one can *answer his arguments*. In a passage recalling the night vision of Eliphaz (4.12–21), though with a different intent, he says that God gives warnings to sinners in an attempt to turn them from their evil ways. Suffering is another warning sent by God, who brings a man near to death but holds him back from the brink in order to discipline him.

33.23–25 Elihu accepts the possibility of heavenly mediators (so many that there need be no fear that some individual may miss their aid). When the sinner is on the edge of death God will send an interpreter who will both *expound God's righteousness to man* and *speak on his behalf*.[2] The mediator not only intercedes on behalf of the sinner but offers a ransom for him. This is a striking advance on anything we have yet seen in the book of Job. The psalmist had said that 'no one can ever ransom himself, nor pay God the price for his release' (Ps. 49.7).[3] Elihu does not say what the ransom is. It appears to purchase an extension of life for the sufferer, and his renewed health and vigour are described in the next verse.

33.26–30 The onus remains on the sinner, however. He must still entreat God *to let him enter his presence*, and openly confess his wrongdoing. Despite the non-Israelite setting of Job, the book reflects many features of Israel's religion and morality. God's presence is probably to be found in the temples, as the psalmist sings, and like the psalmist the sinner's confession is made before the assembled congregation (cf. Pss. 106.6; 116.14). He will then save himself from death. So confident is Elihu of God's mercy that he declares that God will repeatedly accept the repentance of the sinner and restore him *again and again*.

33.31–33 The speech ends incoherently. Elihu tells Job to be silent and allow him to speak, then urges him to answer his arguments if he has anything to say, and before he has a chance to utter a word

---

[2] So REB interprets. But 'God' is not in the text, which reads 'his', and the following line has been transposed from v. 26. The unchanged text might mean that the 'interpreter' sets out what the individual should do if he is to live an upright life.
[3] So REB, adopting the reading of some Hebrew mss. The standard text reads as RV, 'None of them can by any means redeem his brother'.

says that if he has nothing to say he should listen to the wisdom he is going to teach him. Once again the picture of Elihu that we are given is of a self-centred, over-ardent enthusiast, with all the confidence of youth, certain that no one can have any reply to his reasoning.

It is easy to laugh at Elihu, and if his speeches come from our poet it may well be that this was part of his intention. If he inserted ch. 28 to provide a pause before Job's final statement of his case, he may have introduced Elihu as a foil to the divine speeches. We are still uncertain whether we should write Elihu off as merely uttering stale arguments with wearisome repetition, for some of the things he has said have made us pause and ponder. It will be well to withhold our judgment until we have come to the end of what he has to say.

34 Elihu's second speech

Without giving Job an opportunity to respond, Elihu presses on. He condemns Job for denying that God rules the world justly, and after reaffirming that God punishes the wicked according to their deserts, he urges Job to repent. The Hebrew is difficult in several places and scholars differ in their reconstructions and exegesis. As usual we shall follow REB's interpretation.

34.2–4 Either with a sarcastic address to the friends, or appealing to the bystanders, Elihu once again calls upon them to listen to what he has to say. Together they will seek out the truth of the matter.

34.5–9 With a mixture of direct quotation and summary of Job's words, he sets out Job's position as he understands it. Job had accused God of denying him justice (27.2), and had often asserted his innocence. *Was there ever a man like Job with his thirst for irreverent talk?* asks Elihu. He then accuses Job (falsely) of associating with wicked men (cf. Ps. 1.1 for the idea of going on a journey with bad company), and (rightly) of saying that good and bad are treated alike by God (cf. 9.22; 21.7–26).

34.10–15 Again referring to his hearers in flattering or ironical words, Elihu asserts that God *requites everyone according to his actions.* Retribution is exactly meted out. God is just and so it is impossible for him to *pervert justice*. Thus Job's anguished striving to understand why he is suffering so greatly when he knows that he has committed no wrong commensurate with his punishment is brushed aside by a dogmatic repetition of the orthodox creed. Job had refused to excuse God from responsibility for the management of the world (cf. ch. 9). Elihu equally accepts that God is the creator and all living beings derive their life from him, but since he has his preconceived ideas of divine justice, he flatly denies that God ever plays false. Job will not deny his own experience; Elihu closes his eyes to the special situation of Job and the prosperity of blatant sinners.

34.16–28   Turning now to Job, and yet again calling for his close attention, Elihu asks whether it is conceivable that the world should be in the hands of a being who hates justice. On the contrary, God is totally impartial, never showing favour to the rich and powerful but suddenly destroying the wicked in a moment.[1] God keeps watch on everyone and knows all their evil deeds. No one can hide from him. He does not need to hold a special assize to determine their guilt for he sees it immediately. The cry of the poor reaches him and he *strikes down* their oppressors.

34.29–30   Verses 29–30 are obscure. REB has rearranged the words and made other changes to get the sense that, since God is in supreme control, no one dare find fault with the way he rules the world.

34.31–33   Elihu then presses Job to decide whether he would wish God to accept a penitent. If Job were to confess his sin and humble himself before him, resolving never to repeat his sin, does he think that God would *condone* the way he has rejected him?

34.34–37   He appears to think that Job is bound to say that God should pardon the one who is truly contrite, and by making this reply will admit that he should confess his rebellion against God and seek forgiveness. Whether this was his intention or not, true to his character he does not pause for an answer. All sensible men must agree that Job has been talking nonsense. His *endless ranting against God* shows that he is *a sinner and a rebel, a mischief-maker* whom God should silence by bringing him to court *once and for all*.

How differently Job and Elihu perceive the world! Job will not renounce his integrity even if a false confession might give him ease.

---

[1] It is possible that v. 20 stresses the frailty of all God's creatures, even the most powerful, rather than describing God's punishment (as in 8.13–19; 18.5–21; 20.5–1).

He cannot understand why he suffers or why things work out as they do, but he will neither go against his conscience nor deny divine responsibility. Cries of distress, pleas and arguments addressed to his friends, and prayers to God mingle in his speeches. Elihu is supremely confident of his own abilities. He knows exactly how God runs the world. Assured that his creed is true, he can only reassert it and call upon Job to fit his life into its mould. So he addresses bystanders, the friends, and Job, never waiting for a reply and never thinking of praying to God.

35 Elihu continues his argument

35.2–4 In his third speech Elihu picks up several ideas that Job and the friends have put forward, sometimes giving them a different sense. His argument is that God is not touched by either the goodness or the wickedness of human beings. Their actions only affect their fellows. If those who are oppressed receive no answer to their calls to God it is because they have not cried to him aright.

Job has maintained his innocence, but has not asked what benefit he would obtain if he had sinned. Elihu has totally mistaken Job's position. Job like Elihu has expected goodness to be rewarded and cannot understand why he should be suffering as he is. Elihu suggests that what Job is really saying is that, since God makes no distinction between the righteous and sinners, he might as well have sinned. So, with his usual self-confidence, he states that he will *bring arguments* in reply both to him and to the friends.

35.5–8 Job, Eliphaz and Zophar had pointed to the skies to indicate God's greatness and distance from men and women (9.8–12; 11.7–9; 22.12), and Job had asked God how his sin had affected him (7.20). Elihu agrees, and goes on to say that what people do affects only their *fellow-creatures* (cf. Eliphaz, 22.2–3). Job's goodness brings no benefit to God.

35.9–13 The oppressed do cry out to God, but he does not answer because they are *proud and wicked*. Their wickedness seems to consist partly in their unwillingness to acknowledge God's power and wisdom, but the sense of vv. 10–11 is obscure. Job had said that the animals and birds could instruct his friends, but Elihu turns this into a commonplace.

35.14   Verse 14 stands on its own as a direct address to Job between vv. 9–13 and 15–16. As REB interprets it, Elihu appeals briefly to Job to *humble* himself before God and await his revelation. He introduces this with the unkind remark that God does not listen to the oppressed because they have not sought him aright, so there is still less likelihood that he will take notice of him.

35.15–16   Turning back to the friends, or perhaps the bystanders, Elihu says that Job's impious babbling springs from the fact that God has not punished him yet for his *folly*. In 21.14ff Job had declared that the wicked go unpunished, and Elihu may be referring to this, arguing that this is blasphemy, with the implication that it explains Job's sufferings.

   The argument is not coherent, and the figure who is presented to us is of a self-confident young man, who is beginning to run out of original ideas and is picking up only partially understood fragments from the earlier debate.

36–37   The final speech of Elihu

In many places the Hebrew text of Elihu's last speech is even more difficult than the earlier ones. By resorting to emendation, new meanings, and transpositions of verses and lines REB has produced a reasonable sense.

36.2–4   With renewed confidence in his own wisdom and ability, Elihu asks Job to be patient a little longer, for he has still more to say on God's behalf. He is going to range widely in his search for a theodicy which will justify God's actions.

36.5–15   At the beginning and end of the next section of his argument Elihu presents the orthodox doctrine of retribution. God *does* punish the wicked and secure justice for those who have been wronged. Righteous sufferers are raised to positions of esteem alongside kings. If they then fall from favour and suffer as prisoners, this is not punishment but a discipline to show them that they have lapsed into proud and sinful ways. They should listen to God's correction, turn back, and serve him. Then they will live out the rest of their life in comfort and prosperity. Those who do not accept God's discipline will die young and in their prime.

36.16–19   Having set out his beliefs, Elihu applies them to Job, though his words hardly fit Job's present condition. He must not allow bribery to deflect him from dealing out fair justice. He must accept his discipline and not imagine that his wealth can save him.

36.20–37.18   Elihu then turns away from the immediate argument of retribution and the discipline of suffering to proclaim the majestic power of God. His words have often been compared to the divine speeches, with their descriptions of the wonders of nature. Even if similar things are being said, who says them makes a vast difference to their meaning. Elihu urges Job to submit to God's chastisement, for God is almighty: when God speaks to Job out of 'the tempest', it is the same all-powerful deity, but Job is satisfied because he has met God and has not just heard about him at second hand. Elihu stresses that *God is so great that we cannot know him*. Job confesses to God that he had spoken about God out of a lack of knowledge, yet he does now know God, for he has revealed himself to him. Elihu urges Job to *sing the praises of* God's *work*. Job gazes in awe at God's works and reverences God himself the more. Elihu's emphasis is placed upon God's deeds – the rain-storm, the thunder, the flashes of lightning, the snow and ice, which strike terror to the heart of every human being, but we miss any deep longing to draw close to the God who acts in these ways. In the end the listing of natural wonders has only one purpose – to support Elihu's claim that the God who controls these awesome natural forces also has control over the punishment and disciplining of men and women. Even when he puts to Job a similiar *Do you know* to that of God, it is with a different intent.

37.19–24   So in the end Elihu can only ask Job in bitter irony, *Teach us what to say to* God. No one can dictate to God. No one can even find God. Yet despite these avowals of ignorance Elihu can affirm with supreme confidence: *in his great righteousness he does not pervert justice*. So the hidden God is not so darkly concealed after all – at least not to men like Elihu!

We need to return to the question of the place of the Elihu speeches in the book of Job. Let us go over again the arguments of the scholars.

From our twentieth-century perspective it is easy to argue against their authenticity. The folk story tells of only three friends, both before and after the dialogue. The way Elihu addresses Job and the 'three men' is different from the manner of the main cycles of speeches. Elihu is introduced with a repetitious narrative that is matched by repetitious speeches, and this may be the mark of a less gifted writer than our poet. Those who are wise in such matters tell us that the Hebrew style differs from that of the original poet: certainly there seem to be more words that have an Aramaic rather than a Hebrew meaning here. Most of all, it would accord with our dramatic sense if God appeared immediately after Job's appeal to him in the closing verses of ch. 31. Elihu seems to be an interruption.

How conclusive are these arguments?

Everything depends upon our prior ideas. At the most basic level is the supposition that Hebrew writings were edited and re-edited by scribes who introduced their own additions and changes into the text. It may be so, but we do not know. The Chronicler appears to have made changes in narratives which he took over from the books of Samuel and Kings, but even if these were one of his sources he rewrote the narratives into his own quite distinct book. The book of Proverbs is certainly a compilation of earlier and later collections of proverbs and instructions, but the formation of that book is not identical with what is being suggested for the book of Job.

The failure to mention Elihu in the folk story beginning of the book is strange, and his absence from last chapter of the book is extremely odd. Elihu suddenly appears from the group of listeners to the debate and merges into the background as suddenly as he appeared. But who can tell whether this was out poet's intention? If he intended Elihu as a caricature (and this also we do not know) then it might well be part of his purpose to make this opinionated young man thrust himself into the inner circle of friends and then withdraw without waiting either for Job to make any answer or for God to appear. It might well be part of the author's purpose to depict Elihu as one who did not expect God to speak to humans, else why is he so insistent that he has to say so many things 'on God's behalf'? And God's failure to mention Elihu when he tells Eliphaz to go with his two friends and seek Job's prayers may have been intended by our poet to indicate that the failure of this angry young man to show his sympathy with Job by sitting for seven days with him on the refuse heap outside the city put him beyond the reach of even Job's prayers.

As for the interruption between Job's appeal to God and God's answer, again we are forced back to the intentions of our poet and the difficult questions of dramatic sense. Chapters 29–31 match ch. 3, and the cycles of speeches appear to have been skilfully designed with a keen eye for structure. We might well suppose that all that could be said has been said. Only God can contribute anything more. Job's self-assured appeal to God must surely have been answered by God himself – and at this point.

Yet can we be sure? The elaborate introduction of Elihu and the emphasis upon his anger may reveal the mind of our poet. He probably had many different aims in taking up the folk story and filling it with his poetry, one of which may have been to show the utter poverty of every attempt to explain the meaning of suffering. Only by allowing this brash young man to admit that the friends had not produced any answer to Job and then by showing that the young man's arguments were even less telling than theirs could he convince his readers of this fact.

Or he may have held that the stock arguments that we regularly set out to comfort the sufferer and reassure the pious were not totally false. Attitudes mattered more than arguments, however, and by presenting three speakers who were initially sympathetic to Job and one who was not he revealed how fervently he believed this.

Or perhaps he had a very good sense of the dramatic. By presenting a silent God up to the very last moment he pointed to the most mysterious feature about the righteous rule of the world by the righteous God. Eliphaz believed that God would reveal his teaching to human beings – but through a ghostly messenger in the darkness of the night. The other two friends were not concerned whether he revealed himself or not, because they were convinced that what they said was true, based as it was upon tradition and experience. Job had repeatedly asked God to meet him and allow him to vindicate himself, but God had remained silent (9.3, 14, 32–35; 13.3, 15–23; 16.18–22; 19.24–27), and Elihu did not believe that God would ever break his silence, so that he was under immense necessity to refute Job and justify God's rule of the world. Only Job, silent before Elihu's onslaught, refused to believe that God would remain silent for ever.

We can never know what the original intention of our poet was or what his poem looked like when he had completed his work upon it. The text we have in our Hebrew and Greek Bibles is all that we have. But to make sense of the translation that REB places before us is not impossible.

38.1–40.5 *God's first speech and Job's first submission*

'God's answer and Job's submission' is the REB heading to the section 38.1–42.6, but God makes two speeches and Job submits twice. There has been much discussion over this section. Three questions stand out. Why does God continue pressing Job once he has admitted his fault? Why is there such a difference between the pointed, ironic questions in chs. 38–39 and the long description of the crocodile in ch. 41?[1] What is the purpose of the appearance of God, since he does not seem to offer any answer to the problem of suffering and what he says bears no relation to the wager in the first two chapters of the book? This last problem will be left for a general discussion of the meaning of the book. The other two questions can be taken together. Some scholars delete the descriptions of the whale and the crocodile (and possibly the ostrich as well) and combine the two submissions of Job. This certainly improves the climax of the book to our ways of thinking by producing a single divine speech consisting solely of questions to which Job offers a single submission. But we cannot be certain that modern ideas of style and dramatic effect were shared by our poet. To assume that a later editor added the verses in question and so produced Job's double submission reflects a wish to credit our poet with modern sensitivities and to blame the supposed editor for features that do not appeal to us. At a first reading, at least, we should try to understand the book as it lies before us.

God in the book of Job is a powerful and transcendent deity, and the *tempest* emphasizes this. Older translations uses 'whirlwind', which has even more terrifying overtones. We need to put away all thoughts of the rather sentimental 'fatherhood' of God which have become common in modern Christianity. God in Job is the omnipotent and omniscient creator.

38.1–3 God's first words to Job are harsh. Job is addressed as one who lacks *knowledge* and whose arguments have muddied intelligent thought. To convince him that this is so, God says he will put hard questions to which he must answer if he can.

God's speech divides into four sections in which God directs Job's attention to many natural phenomena which Job cannot explain: the creation of the world (38.4–11), wonders of the heavens (38.12–21), meteorological features (38.22–38), and finally a series of wild animals, lions (38.39–40), ravens (38.41), mountain goats (39.1–4), the wild ass (39.5–8), the wild ox (39.9–12), the ostrich (39.13–18), the war horse (39.19–25), birds of prey (39.26–30), and the whale (41.1–6).

To understand the description of creation we need to forget everything which modern astonomers have taught us about the

---

[1] REB has moved 41.1–6 to follow 39.30 and treated it as a description of the whale, leaving the whole of 40.15–41.34 as the crocodile. We shall consider the identifications as we come to them.

expanding universe, and put from our minds that wonderful photograph of the fragile blue sphere which is our earth that space research has given us. The writer of Job accepted the science of his own day, a science which took its origins from what the world looks like if we simply use our eyes and then try to make sense of what we see. The earth is a flat plate, supported by pillars. The sky is a solid dome which makes a space for humans and the animals to inhabit in the midst of the surrounding waters that produce springs and rain. It is a picture of the world which was common to many peoples of the ancient Middle East, although in some ways the writer of Job had a more sophisticated view than we find in some other places in the Old Testament. (See Gen. 1 for an elaborate and hymn-like account, and Pss. 24.1–2; 104; 136.5–9; Prov. 8.27–29; and Isa. 40.12, 21–22 for poetic glimpses of this cosmology.)

38.4–7   How can Job understand how God rules the universe when he was not present at its creation? He does not know its *dimensions* and cannot say what supports the pillars upon which the earth rests. 38.7 is one of the most marvellous verses in the whole Old Testament, expressing the wonder and joy at the universe which God created. No humans yet exist to delight in God's new creation, so it is left to the *morning stars* and the members of God's heavenly court to sing aloud in songs of joy. The writer of Prov. 8 makes wisdom the sole companion of God at the creation, although it is not certain what her role is, whether as a little child playing while the world was made and delighting in everything she sees, or as the master-craftsman responsible for fashioning the universe (Prov. 8.22–31, see REB mg. on v. 30).

38.8–11   In several of the myths that were known in the ancient Middle East the Sea is one of the opponents of the creator God. In the Old Testament there are hints of this in several psalms (cf. Pss. 29.10; 46.3; 93.1–4). People in those times knew both the destructiveness of the waters in flood and the vital necessity of water for all living things to survive. The picture of the creation of the waters in REB here is not clear. Is it a birth scene with the sea bursting out of the womb of some goddess, being *supported* by God as a midwife might take up the newly born child and carefully wrap it up, mist being the *blanket* in which the sea is enfolded; but then suddenly the midwife God realizes that the new-born sea is a dangerous monster and sets strict limits its sway? Or are two metaphors or myths combined, a birth myth and a separate myth of the barring of the advance of the sea by strong gates? Whatever may have contributed to our poet's thought, he has presented a wonderful picture of the power of the sea and the even greater power of God.

38.12–15 From the first moments of creation, our poet turns to the starlit heavens. The description of the dawn is a splendid personification. Again precisely what was in the mind of our poet is not certain. At one point the dawn seems to be reaching to the *fringes* of a blanket which covers the earth and then *shaking* out the stars. The image changes and the growing light allows the contours of the hills and valleys to be seen like the impressions made by a *seal* in the *clay* which receives its imprint, or like the *folds* of a cloak. Then imagery is abandoned and our poet describes the fading of the *Dog-star* and the *stars of the Navigator's Line*[2] as the light brightens.

38.16–21 From the heights of the stars our poet drops to the depths of the primeval ocean (the same word as in Gen. 1.2) and the land of the dead below this. The *springs* are the sources of the seas. The abode of the dead is pictured, as in Babylon, as a city with gates, and so with *door-keepers*. *Light* and *darkness* are another measure of the immensity of the universe. The picture is similar to that in Gen. 1, where there is primordial darkness and light is the first of God's creations. We need not suppose that our poet was unaware that light comes from the sun. He is using poetic and perhaps mythological images. Casting his glance across the longest reaches of time and space, God asks Job if he has travelled to these far places and comprehended their vast expanse, and with irony suggests that he must have been present when the world was made, for his speeches lay claim to such vast knowledge.

38.22–30 Possibly continuing the same voyage through the natural world, or perhaps moving to new regions of climate and weather, God ruthlessly pursues his questioning. *Snow* and *hail* are pictured as being stored up, ready to be sent out upon the earth. The link with war perhaps reflects the Israelite idea that God used the storm to defeat Israel's enemies (cf. Josh. 10.11; Judg. 5.20–21; Ps. 18.11–15; Isa. 30.30). The *heat* and *east wind* refer to the burning wind which

---

[2] REB accepts the identification of the first Hebrew word (amended slightly, see mg.) as the *Dog-star*, Canis major, and the second (literally 'uplifted arm') as the line of stars stretching like a bent arm from the horizon to the Zenith and passing through Sirius, Procyon, Castor and Pollux. This retains the astronomical references throughout the section.

sweeps across the hot desert and dries up everything living. Rain is sometimes pictured in the Old Testament as the opening up of sluices in the dome of the sky (Gen. 7.11; II Kings 7.19; Isa. 24.18). Later in this chapter the clouds appear to be compared to water-skins which are tilted and their water emptied on the earth (38.37, cf. Ps. 147.8)). In v. 25 our poet speaks of conduits or trenches along which the rain flows (the word is used of the conduit which Hezekiah had dug to bring water into Jerusalem, II Kings 20.20). To stress that his actions reach beyond the regions which human beings know, God adds that he sends rain upon *uninhabited* deserts and even there makes plants grow. In poetic metaphor he asks whether Job knows who is the *father* of the rain or the *mother* of the ice and frost.

38.31–34   Verses 31–33a might appear to interrupt the account of the weather. REB seems to place the emphasis upon the production of rain. The argument would then be that Job's inability to construct the laws which govern the stars is matched by his inability to produce rain. This reveals his lack of understanding and power.

38.35–38   With v. 35 we return to the description of the storm. The lightning will not wait until Job tells it to strike, and it is not his command which makes the clouds release their rain. Verse 36 is very difficult and the translation which REB adopts is something of an aside and would seem to pick up the idea that Job does not understand the cosmic wisdom by which the universe is governed for he did not devise it.

38.39–41   The description of the physical world ended, God turns to the animal kingdom. The lion was regarded as the most fearsome and self-reliant of beasts. It does not need humans to find its prey (cf. Ps. 104.21–22). Ravens seem to have fascinated the ancient Israelites, and Job is again one with the psalmists who tell of the divine origin of their food (cf. Ps. 147.9).

39.1–12   The questions in the next three sections fasten upon the wildest of creatures, so different from the animals which ancient peoples had tamed: mountain goats, wild asses, and the *wild ox* (possibly the aurochs). The television brings to us the mysteries of the natural world which naturalists have not only uncovered but have succeeded in recording in picture and sound. Once again we need to put this knowledge behind us and gaze out at the world from the eyes of ancient men and women. The length of the pregnancy of the domestic animals was presumably known, and shepherds would certainly have attended the birth of lambs. By contrast the shy mountain goats were outside ordinary acquaintance and comprehension. The wild ass kept far from the towns and, roaming free, did not have to obey any driver. The wild ox was very different from the oxen who pulled the plough for the peasants in every country of the ancient Middle East – strong but untamable, impossible to use for ploughing or as a draught animal.

39.15–18   The description of the ostrich[3] differs from the rest of the divine speech in chs. 38–39 in that it is not in the form of a series of questions, and God is referred to in v. 17 in a way that is strange in a divine speech. The section is missing from the ancient Greek translation. These three facts have suggested to some scholars that these verses were added to the speech by a later writer. REB shows no hesitations. The ostrich was clearly regarded as a very peculiar kind of bird, with *stunted* wings, proverbial for its failure to build a proper nest and care for its eggs or young, and yet able to outpace a horse. Among the many and varied senses of 'wisdom' in Job, here the wilful negligence of the ostrich is seen as showing a lack of this virtue, a failing so contrary to normal instinct that it can be attributed only to God's direct intention.

39.19–25   The description of the war horse is one of the finest in the whole book, well rendered in REB. Attempts to 'explain' such poetry can only reveal the incompetence of the interpreter. The picture of the mighty, quivering beast, eager to enter the fray is open to any reader.

39.26–30   Birds of prey, like lions and the wild creatures of the wilderness, also fascinated the ancients. Their keen sight was legendary, their inaccessible nests aroused admiration, their love of carrion called forth disgust and horror – and interest too. They needed no human teachers.

At this point REB inserts 41.1–6, part of the section of God's second speech which describes 'Leviathan'. Questions of authenticity and interpretation are raised.

1. In the Hebrew the second divine speech consists of an introduction (40.7–14) and then the descriptions of two animals, Behemoth

[3] This is certainly the bird that is in view, despite the uncertainty about the precise name (cf. mg.).

(40.15–25) and Leviathan (41.1–34). These are much longer than any of the descriptions in the first speech, Leviathan grossly so, and for much of the time they lack the question form that is so characteristic of that speech. Some scholars therefore would simply delete them as additions by a later scribe. 'Behemoth' seems to be out of place in its present position, for God has challenged Job to answer further questions, and questions concerning his just rule of the world to boot, while here we are given a straight description. Moreover, the description of Leviathan is so lengthy that it is totally out of character with the rest of the speeches. Other scholars accept the originality of 41.1–8 as being in question form and suitable to the style and purpose of the speeches.

2. But what creatures did the writer, whoever he was, have in mind? 'Behemoth' looks like the plural of the Hebrew word which normally refers to domestic animals in general, and oxen and cows in particular, though it is sometimes used of wild animals (cf. 40.15, mg.). It might, however, be intended as the name of a particular kind of animal, and although REB treats the passage as a description of the crocodile, most commonly Behemoth is identified as the hippopotamus. By transferring 41.1–6 to the end of ch. 39 REB extends the description of the crocodile to the whole of what is left of 40.15–41.34, and then follows the suggestion that 41.1–6 describe the whale.

This, however, is not the end of the story. Leviathan is the well-known name of a mythological animal, mentioned in the texts from Ugarit and referred to in several places in the Old Testament as we saw when we looked at 3.8. The question is therefore raised, Are both creatures (or maybe just Leviathan), mythological or are they real? REB plumps for reality and this is probably right,[4] even though individual features in the descriptions can be interpreted in a mythological way. There would seem to be no reason for the introduction of mythological creatures at this point.

41.1–6 The section on the whale which is included by REB at the end of ch. 39 follows the pattern of questions asked of Job, suits the theme of the speech in that it introduces yet another creature far different from the normal domestic animals, and is of a length with the accounts of the other creatures. No one is able to catch a whale using normal fishing tackle, it will not become a slave of humans, and no group of fishermen would be likely to join together to try to

---

[4] Though I question the identifications and have doubts about the transposition.

take it, and then haggle over how much each should have. Two delightful touches are added. The whale is not likely to beg for mercy like human captives, and it is too massive to be made a caged animal or kept on a leash for children to play with.

40.1–5 In conclusion God asks Job whether he has any answer now, and Job's response is an admission that he has no more to say. No particular stress should be placed upon the *once* and *twice*; this is a common form of repetition in poetic parallelism in the Old Testament and elsewhere, for example at Ugarit. Job is simply stating that before this majestic and transcendent God he is totally insignificant.

40.6–42.6 God's second speech; Job says he is satisfied

The introduction to God's second speech is identical to 38.1, and the speech begins similarly (cf. 38.3). Job has dared to claim that God's rule of the world is unjust. So God invites him to take control and see if he can run it any better. But he points out that he does not have the power to enforce his will, and his criticisms are therefore futile.

The rest of ch. 40 and the whole of ch. 41 is taken by REB as a description of the crocodile, following an emendation and fresh interpretation of v. 15 and the removal of 41.1–6. As we have already seen, there is no need to regard this as a mythological monster, although some features might just possibly have been derived from such a source. This is a real crocodile. There are many unusual words in these verses, and although the general meaning is relatively clear, REB has had to resort to emendations and new meanings to produce sense in some places. There is no direct repetition, but the poet moves back and forth and the description cannot usefully be subdivided. In any case the picture which he draws is vivid and clear.

40.15–41.34 The poet stresses the great strength of the crocodile, pointing to his massive frame and the way he can devour cattle and wild animals as if they were grass. He is too powerful for men to seize, his armour resists all weapons, his teeth are terrible, and he invokes great fear in those who would hunt him. The statement that *Firebrands shoot from his mouth* has persuaded some scholars that it is the mythological Leviathan who is being described, but so much of the rest of the account is realistic that this is probably to be explained as poetic imagery.

42.1–6   Job now makes his second submission. REB has identified the first half of 42.3 and most of 42.4 as quotations of God's address to Job by inserting *You said* (cf. 38.2, 3; 40.7). This is needed in translation for clarity. Job acknowledges God's power (which he had never questioned) but now accepts that he has criticized his rule of the world without possessing an understanding of the way God maintained that rule. He still has no greater knowledge, yet he confesses himself satisfied. He has met God at last. It is not a matter of debating an abstract theology. Experience has replaced intellectual striving. So he submits. *Repent* in English implies admission of guilt. This is not a necessary component of the meaning of the Hebrew word, and we should be false to Job if we believed that he had at last accepted the advice of the friends and gone back on his conviction of his moral integrity. He admits he was wrong in questioning God's rule of the world. He does not concede that he has committed any sin that would merit such suffering as has come to him.

42.7–17   *The epilogue*

The book ends, as it began, with a narrative in prose. God tells Eliphaz that he is angry with him and the other two friends because they have not spoken about him rightly as Job has done. They are to offer sacrifices and ask Job to pray for them. Job's prosperity is then restored, with double the number of livestock and the same number of sons and daughters. The beauty of the daughters is extolled and, unusually, the writer gives their names and adds that they were given a share in the family inheritance. (In Israel daughters could only inherit property and goods if there were no sons (Num. 21.1–11), although in other countries of the ancient Middle East, and among a group of Jews in Egypt, women could possess property in their own right.) Oddly nothing is said about Job's return to full health, but this is clearly implied. His brothers and sisters, who have not been mentioned before, come to comfort him and bring him gifts.[1] Job lives to see his great grandchildren and dies, as a righteous man should, in a good old age (cf. 5.25–26; 29.13–20).

[1] The mg. 'piece of money' is perhaps preferable to 'sheep'. What need would Job have of one or two extra sheep when he has fourteen thousand sheep and goats? True, he would not need the money either, but the coin and the ring are token gifts.

And here is the problem for many readers. Does not this ending destroy all that has been argued in the dialogue? Is this not what the friends had said would happen if only Job would repent and submit to God? Is not this the false doctrine which Job had believed equally with the friends and against which he had rebelled because he refused to deny his integrity?

Again we need to try to take ourselves back into the world of the Old Testament. This life is all. Death is the end. Any vindication must be worked out in this world. Hence if God is to be seen as acknowledging that Job was in the right he has to show his favour in the present. Any judge who left a defendant to languish in prison after he had been declared innocent would be condemned as unjust.

This is not all that is to be said. The restoration of Job's fortunes is not a 'reward' for good behaviour. It is *restoration*, even if it goes beyond what Job possessed at the beginning. The trial of Job's faith is complete. Some scholars emphasize that it is a gift of grace. God's confidence in Job has been vindicated against the Satan's cynicism. The drama is ended.

For Job, however, it had ended earlier. Once he had met God face to face he declared himself satisfied, even though he had found no answers to his questions concerning the justice of his treatment and the righteousness of God's government of the world.

What then was the purpose of our poet in composing his book? To this we must now turn.

II

The Author's Purpose

If we only possessed the prose sections of the book its meaning might seem to be fairly clear. The author rejects the orthodox teaching about reward and punishment and offers the explanation that suffering is a test of faith.

Questions quickly arise, however. Is the writer's purpose really to undermine the orthodox theory? What he tells is the story of one righteous man: can we be sure that he intended to assert that *all* suffering is to be explained in the same way? Job is depicted as completely blameless, almost too good to be true: might he not accept that the orthodox teaching about reward and punishment applies to the general run of men and women, though not to such a man as Job?

There are few hints in the story itself that the writer is concerned with any 'theory of retribution', orthodox or otherwise; At the first meeting of the heavenly council God simply points out that in Job he has found one perfectly good man, while the Satan's response is to argue that Job has been so protected by God that he has 'good reason to be God-fearing'. It is true that in the second encounter between God and the Satan God speaks of ruining Job 'without cause', but this is still far short of affirming a far-reaching system of punishments, though it perhaps reflects a feeling that there should be some correlation between goodness and prosperity. The infliction of running sores is no more than an extension of the first test. At this stage Job does not make any link between suffering and sin: evil is to be accepted from God in just the same way as good, with no suggestion that either is a recompense for virtue or wrong-doing. Job's wife tells him to 'Curse God, and die!', but this need not be extended to mean that evil deeds will be punished by death. Cursing God is to renounce God, to reject his rule, to blaspheme. God might well bring about the death of the man who repudiated him in this way; it need not imply a system of retribution fitted exactly to every deed.

The test, then, does not necessarily relate to the theology of reward and punishment which we found in the Deuteronomistic history, in Proverbs and several Psalms, and in some of the sayings of the prophets. On this reading, Job is a perfectly just man whose goodness is matched by his trust in God and his faithful performance of religious duties. The Satan questions whether he would retain his integrity if life were harsher, and God permits the double test. Job comes out of the ordeal with his trust in God unflawed.

With this reading the concluding narrative agrees. The test is over. God is vindicated. The Satan's cynicism is shown to be false. Job can now receive back his wealth. Seven sons and three beautiful daughters complete his blessing.

There is much of value here. For a faith to be genuine it must be possible to doubt God, to be able to say, 'This I will do and this I will stand to, whatever the consequence may be.' Only so is the highest goodness possible. A world where goodness is always rewarded would be the Satan's world and not God's. We may reject the idea that God tests his faithful servants, but we must accept that he has created a world in which the good may not live out all his days in prosperity and health. The way the wicked often flourish may be left on one side for the moment. For the highest kind of faith and goodness it must at least be possible for there to be Jobs in the world.

So much might be said if the narrative stood on its own. But it does not. Our poet has told the story to introduce the dialogue. Even if he took a folk story as the basis of his work, he has retold it. The friends are introduced. At the end they are rebuked. Job's goodness is reaffirmed by his restoration to prosperity and also by his prayer for the friends, prayer that is heard by God. We need to look at the book as a whole. And taking the book as a whole makes it impossible to accept some interpretations which scholars have proposed.

There is, for example, the view that the teaching on suffering which our poet wishes to present is that expressed by the friends. Which of the friends, we need to ask first?

Suffering is punishment, say all the friends, and then with relentless logic they argue that Job must be a great sinner because he suffers so greatly. This is clearly not true, and it is inconceivable that our poet accepted this doctrine. Whatever he may or may not have intended to teach through his poem, his constant reiteration of Job's goodness, and the final condemnation of the three friends by God are sufficient for us to reject this idea out of hand. Moreover, he shows that the only way in which the friends can make this dogma work out is to assert that Job must be a great sinner because he suffers so greatly. Their logic is faulty. Even if sin led to punishment, it does not follow that when a man suffers he is by this very suffering marked out as a great sinner. Sin often does bring suffering. It does not mean that suffering is always and only caused by sin. Our poet, however, may not have been greatly interested in logic. It was enough for him that Job was cleared by God and by his own conscience. The book makes no sense unless we accept that Job is indeed a blameless man.

Suffering is a discipline, said Eliphaz, and Elihu picked up the idea and extended it. Job is a good man, but he should have accepted the suffering meekly (as he had done in the prologue). His passionate outbursts are blameworthy. If only he would submit to God, then God would accept him and all would be well again.

We find it a little difficult to understand how discipline can apply to a someone who is perfectly righteous. Those who have committed small sins may be brought back to the way of goodness through chastisement, but to discipline a man who both God and the Satan agree has no faults looks too much like using pain as a deterrent before any wrong is committed, like holding the child's fingers against the hot bars to teach it not to go near the fire.

Yet we must always be on our guard lest we read into the Old Testament ideas which come from our very different age. In itself the belief is not impossible. Our poet may have hinted at discipline in that early speech by Eliphaz, and then introduced Elihu to confirm that this was his final word. The speeches by God add nothing to the argument after Elihu has spoken. Suffering is discipline and warning, and all his readers would do well to pay heed when suffering comes, he may have intended to say.

Now it is true that God does not rebuke Elihu. He ignores him, however, and by this our poet probably implies that he has rejected his exhortations and his philosophy. It is true that God does not offer any alternative theory to explain why men and women suffer, but our poet may have had other reasons for introducing God into his poem than giving the answer to the 'problem of suffering'. We need still to keep an open mind.

If our poet did not intend the three friends and Elihu to set out his own view of suffering, perhaps he introduced them with the opposite purpose. They declare the theory of suffering which he wishes to refute. Job is perfectly righteous. The friends are wrong in accusing him of secret sins. Maybe the friends are wrong in even greater matters. Their whole conception of the link between sin and suffering, the whole edifice of reward and punishment has to be destroyed. What better way of doing this than by showing that it does not fit the case of one righteous man. The experience of Job is enough. The old orthodoxy can no longer be believed.

It seems a negative attitude. Has our poet set out his three cycles of speeches, brought in Elihu, affirmed that Job is blameless, introduced God himself, given his story a fairy-tale ending, and never once offered to his readers any explanation of why human beings suffer as they do? Surely, if his purpose was to produce a theodicy he must be adjudged to have failed. Not in this way is it possible to justify God's ways to man.

There is value in clearing the ground. If an accepted dogma is false, the first essential is to show its error and sweep it out of the way. So long as it is believed there will be no incentive to create a better theory, and many will remain in their blindness. If, therefore, our poet leaves us simply with a reverent agnosticism, that at least is an advance upon the old mistaken theology.

Searching in the speeches of the friends and of Elihu will not lead to the discovery of our poet's teaching. And yet not everything which they say is false. Wrong doing can lead to suffering – the suffering of others even if not the suffering of the sinner himself. We are all bound up in the bundle of life, and what one person does spills over into the lives of those who are near. The prophet may reject the proverb, 'The fathers have eaten sour grapes and the children's teeth are set on edge',[1] but many children know the bitterness of the inheritance that has come down to them. There are occasions when the consequence of the misuse of one's body is the disease that attacks that same body. There have been times when a wicked man seems to be doing well, and suddenly disaster strikes. But equally there are other evil men and women who enjoy health and rich prosperity, whose oppression of the poor only increases their power and wealth, who seem able to laugh at illness and live to a ripe old age. When they die they are surrounded by their children and grandchildren and held in honour within their community. And the experience of Job proclaims with a force that will not brook contradiction, even though the friends attempt to do so, that sometimes a perfectly righteous man suffers hideously.

May it perhaps be, then, that our poet intended to point to the ambiguity of life? Neither the friends nor Job are completely wrong, none is totally in the right. God evades the question of the meaning of suffering, yet in the end he makes no charge against Job except that he has claimed a knowledge of the way the universe is governed

[1] Jer. 31.29–30; Ezek. 18.2–3.

which is beyond his powers. 'We cannot know', might be the motto of the book.

So far we have assumed that our poet was concerned with the 'problem of suffering'. His purpose was with theodicy, either to reject a false one, or to present a true one, or to show his readers that no human being has the wisdom or knowledge to understand the way God rules his universe. But is this so? It may not have been his aim at all.

Perhaps our poet was more concerned with faith and the way human beings can relate to God than with the more general problems of suffering and theodicy. As we read through the dialogue we find that the emphasis subtly changes. At first Job is simply concerned with his pain and longs for death. His friends are horrified at his plight, but even more appalled at his outburst, yet they sincerely try to bring comfort. Eliphaz points to Job's earlier piety, argues that everyone is sinful, and urges Job to submit to God. Bildad assures him that God will not reject those who are blameless, and reassures Job that he will soon enjoy his former happiness. Zophar repeats the orthodox theology of retribution, although he accepts that God is mysterious and hidden, and like the other friends exhorts Job to repent and thrust his evil from him, for in this way he will find renewed blessing. As we move into the second and third cycle of speeches, we find that the friends continue to reiterate the close connection between morality and retribution, becoming increasingly convinced that Job must be a great sinner to be punished so severely.

Job stands in great contrast to the friends. He, like them, accepts the orthodox theology, but unlike them, he refuses to accept that his punishment shows that he is a great sinner. Whatever else he gives up, he will never relinquish his confidence in his integrity. And it doesn't make sense. Something has gone awry. Somehow God does not seem to know of his righteousness. In his speeches, therefore, he tries to find a way to reach God and present his case. The climax is his final appeal to God in ch. 31. He sets out his innocence that was entirely true and proclaims that any indictment that God might draw up against him would be seen to be a record of such surpassing goodness that he could 'flaunt it on [his] shoulder' and 'wear it like a crown'.

At this point Elihu is an intrusion. What Job wants is to meet God, which is perhaps why he makes no reply to Elihu's questions. When God does appear, however, it is not to present his indictment, nor to declare Job's innocence, but to humble Job before his majesty and power. This was just what Job said would happen (chs. 9–10). Yet oddly Job abases himself before the transcendent God and says that he is satisfied.

Job never abandons the theology which he shared with the friends from the first. Like them he had built his life upon the belief that if he obeyed God then God would reward him. What he now discovered is that morality is not religion. No one, not even the most perfect of men, can approach God with brazen confidence in his record of good deeds.[2] God must be worshipped solely for what he is. The only proper attitude possible before him is reverence and awe. It is not far from what Paul meant by justification by faith.

But have we strayed too far into the ideas of the New Covenant? Perhaps we should look at the book again, this time examining the faith of Job and the friends, rather than turning aside to discuss retribution and the position of men and women before God.

As we have seen, Job and the friends hold that there is a connection between goodness and prosperity. The friends never abandon this faith. For them religion consists of doing what is right. They remain firmly tied to tradition. Experience, and, for Eliphaz, revelation as well, confirm this. The more Job rages, the more confident they are that he is a sinner. As R. Davidson has finely put it, 'If Job's experience does not fit in with the religious script they are following, so much the worse for Job's experience. Their theology insists that Job must have sinned grievously, therefore he has sinned grievously. Rather than revise their script, they are prepared to rewrite Job's life.'[3]

Before the disaster struck Job had held the same faith as the friends. If he had been asked why he believed in God, he would have said, 'How can I *not* believe? Look at my seven thousand sheep, my three thousand camels, my five hundred pairs of oxen, my five hundred donkeys. Look at my seven fine sons and my three beautiful daughters.' Now all that had gone. His sheep had been killed, his camels carried off, his children were dead. The story said that he accepted it all patiently and piously. Yet his first speech showed that this was not so. And as we read on we discover that it is not just his home and his farms that have been destroyed. He can no longer believe in a God who cares, a God who gives blessing to the man who keeps himself blameless. And this uncaring God is too powerful for him to

[2] It is a pity that REB has abandoned the picture of Job striding into God's presence like a prince (cf. 31.37, RSV: 'I would give him an account of all my steps; like a prince I would approach him'), for this is what he is doing.
[3] *The Courage to Doubt*, p. 178. He adds, 'not the first or the last time that truth has been sacrificed upon the altar of deeply-held theological convictions'.

argue with. He can neither find him nor can he believe that he will deign to answer him.

Yet he fights to find a new faith – a faith here and now. No traditional lore will help. No assurance handed on from others will bear him up. Not even the faith that was his in the past is any good now. It must be a faith which accepts the reality of both his own goodness and the disaster that has befallen him. He at any rate is not prepared to rewrite his life in order to retain his piety or whitewash God. He insists on forcing a way through to God, cost what it may.

Is it not striking that while the friends are so confident of their orthodoxy they never once turn to God in prayer? It is the rebellious Job, Job the doubter, who time after time in his speeches turns away from the friends and from his own bitter thoughts to address God.

So Job makes his final appeal – and has to wait while Elihu seeks to put God's case for him. For Elihu does not believe that God will ever speak to human beings. To Elihu he is always a silent God. Then at last God comes to Job in the whirlwind. It is the majestic and transcendent God who speaks. He does overwhelm Job with his power, just as Job had said he would. He does not explain to Job why he is suffering. He says nothing to reassure him that he knows he is innocent. And Job has no answer to his questions. How unsatisfactory it all is! God does not even seem to be satisfied with Job's first submission, and in the book as we now have it batters Job still more with further questions and the portrait of the fearsome crocodile. Yet Job says that he is satisfied.

> I have spoken of things
> which I have not understood,
> things too wonderful for me to know. . . .
> I knew of you then only by report,
> but now I see you with my own eyes.
> Therefore I yield,
> repenting in dust and ashes.

On this reading of the book, we see our poet presenting a man whose faith has been destroyed and whose faith has been restored, though it is a very different faith which he has at the end from that he had at the beginning.

Was it then the purpose of our poet to portray a sufferer battling his way to a personal faith from a faith which had been handed down to him by his parents and the wise men of old? Or is there yet another way of reading this strange and wonderful book?

When we read the heavenly court scene and the account of God's wager with the Satan we asked, What kind of a God is it who will so easily take up the Satan's challenge, and then admit that he allowed himself to be incited by his cynicism to 'ruin [Job] without cause'? Do not God's own words reveal his sense of guilt? What kind of a God is it who would succumb a second time when the stakes were raised? Was not Job's wife right? Should not Job have cursed such a God – even if it took him to his death?

If we read the book with these questions in our minds we discover yet another way of interpreting what our poet was attempting. In a sense it was fair to test Job's integrity. He had been protected. Life had been easy. At no time had he been required to battle against poverty or suffered oppression by the powerful men in his community. He was one of the powerful ones – even though he used his power benignly. So it was fair to probe the strength and character of Job's faith. The Satan was doing no more than his duty, despite his sneering scepticism.

But by taking up the challenge God was showing that the universe is not controlled by moral laws. Goodness does not lead inevitably to prosperity. The wicked are not always punished. Job is right in his complaints. The friends' attempt to make God more righteous than he is fails. And if it is no possible option to limit God's responsibility by making him the God of deism, creator of the universe but no longer coming to human beings to help or punish (and none of the characters will accept this let-out), then the integrity of God's rule must also be tested.

How does this scenario work out? The friends stand firm to their orthodoxy. God's rule is just. The wicked are punished, even if they sometime prosper for a time. The righteous will receive their reward, even though it has to be won through the discipline of chastisement. And Job still does not fit into the scheme.

Job's Archimedes' point is his integrity. Whatever else must be relinquished, this he will not abandon. Here alone can he find leverage to attempt to understand the workings of the world. It can lead only to an unjust God – the God of ruthless power, the spy, the torturer of men and women, the one who hedges in those against whom he sets his face, who gives the world into the hands of the wicked. Job will not flinch from the darkest conclusions.

And yet . . . Job longs for a mediator, longs to be hidden until God's inexplicable anger has passed and he once more has an equal longing for his friend. But it may be too late. His vindication may have to be after his death. There is a faint hope that he might be granted a glimpse – no more – of his acquittal, his rehabilitation, though he is in the land of the dead from which there is no return.

In the end he is granted a glimpse of the way God rules the universe – a rule that is mysterious and hidden from human eyes and minds, a rule that does not touch goodness and evil, a wisdom that belongs to the cosmic forces, not moral law.

All is then restored. The wheel has turned. Prosperity is renewed, and lasts until his death in old age and happiness, although what God has revealed to him gives him no certainty of this.

On this reading we have the strangest book in the whole Bible. It is a book in which there is a human morality that transcends almost everything that we find in the Old Testament, though much can be matched both in the law and the prophets, and some finds parallels in the lands of the Middle East outside of Israel. But this is not the morality by which God rules the world. We have a book which comes so close to blasphemy that it is a wonder that it was not more heavily glossed than parts of it seem to have been, yet which contains passages that express a sense of reverence and awe in the presence of God which are matched only in the Psalter and the Revelation of St John. And we have a book which accepts that at death all human beings go to the land of no return, a land of forgetfulness where the one blessing is that those who are oppressed are eased of their burdens, and yet a book in which longings for a life after death are found, deeper and more spiritual than the easy resurrection of Dan. 12.2, and again finding their kin only in occasional verses in the Psalms.

Here is a questing which refuses bland reassurances, a doubting which retains its hold upon faith, a rebellion which never forswears its allegiance to the God who is worshipped, and a final submission which confesses ignorance but never admits sin.

III

Job: A Twentieth-Century Christian Reading

We have attempted to read the book of Job with attention, sympathy, and imagination, taking REB as one interpretation and eschewing any attempt to improve upon the text the translators adopted or to criticize their translation, for they are wise and learned men and women. During our first reading we cast aside our Christian viewpoint and tried to think as our poet thought in that far-off age and that distant country. With that 'willing suspension of disbelief' we joined Job and his friends, grieving on the heap of ashes outside the city, listening enthralled at speech and counter-speech, filled with awe as Yahweh spoke out of the tempest, happy to see Job's return to prosperity, joyful as we met his seven fine sons and his three beautiful daughters, Jemimah, Keziah, and Kerenhappuch. It is time to turn back to the beginning of the book and read the story and the speeches once more.

But now we read as men and women of the twentieth century. Vast cities with supermarkets replace the little towns of ancient Israel. Light comes from atomic and coal-burning power stations rather than an oil lamp. Cars, trains, and aircraft move with much greater speed than Job's donkeys. In the countryside tractors and combines till the fields and reap the harvest far more rapidly than Job's oxen were able. Science reveals a universe vaster than ever Job could envisage, but the heavens we see are duller, for city lights and polluted air blot out the fainter stars. If we are ill, hospitals with expensive equipment offer organ transplants and intensive care. Social security is a safety-net against the worst poverty. In religion we are offered choices among many denominations and world faiths, and some of the men and women we work with believe in no God at all. Words bombard us on every side. Television fills the hours when Job and his friends were pondering deep questions of life and death and suffering, and God's place in it all. And we who read are women as well as men, conscious that 'man' seems to exclude 'woman', and incensed that the feelings and thoughts of Job's wife were of no concern to our poet, who could make Job dismiss her as talking like 'any impious woman'.

What has our poet to say to us across the centuries and out of so alien a culture?

1   Job 1–2: Why suffering?

Hagiography is out of fashion. Lytton Strachey has done his debunking work. We live in a cynical age. The sole criterion in education as well as business is value for money. We side more naturally with the Satan than with God. 'Has not Job good reason to be godfearing?' Indeed he has. The setting is idyllic. Rich farms permit an endless round of feasting. And when disaster comes we feel that Job ought not to have taken it so lightly. 'The LORD gives and the LORD takes away; blessed be the name of the LORD. . . . If we accept good from God, shall we not accept evil?' We find it difficult to credit such patience and piety. And when our poet tells us that 'Throughout all this Job did not sin, nor did he ascribe any fault to God', and later 'Throughout all this, Job did not utter one sinful word', we are amazed. And in our incredulity we are more cynical than the Adversary himself, for he knew full well that Job was blameless. His unbelief was that any man would maintain his integrity if he were not hedged around on every side with God's protection. He was convinced that piety is only possible in the comfort of prosperity. Is it experience of life in a grasping and violent age that produces a cynicism more disbelieving than the Satan's? Or is it the Christian doctrine of original sin, which has been the ground upon which the Christian scheme of salvation has been erected? Perhaps we should pay more heed to the fact that Jesus spoke of sin but rarely, always took the side of the man or woman who was being accused of wrong, was convinced that goodness was attractive.

On our first reading of Job we saw that unless we take the goodness of Job seriously the book makes no sense. It is because Job is blameless that the problems of suffering and of the relation of men and women to God press upon him.

The problem of suffering is certainly alive today. The more medical science pushes back the frontiers of death and presses the battle against disease, the more we feel that sickness and death are the great evils that afflict mankind. The more the hope of a future life in which wrongs suffered in this life may be righted withers, the more we rebel against all suffering. At least Job, to whom the only future is the gloom of the land of no return, is nearer to our mood than the radiant confidence of the New Testament.

Our approach to the problem, however, is very different from our poet's. We can readily imagine the kind of programme that would be produced on television about the problem of suffering. We should be shown a series of rapid shots of the many different kinds of pain – a cancer patient, a child wounded in Beirut, the victims of a road crash, an aged and senile patient in a geriatric ward, hungry people in Africa, the oppressed in some Latin American country. The dead and wounded in two world wars, Auschwitz, and Hiroshima could not be left out. Then we would be introduced to a panel of 'experts', a sociologist, a psychologist, a philosopher, perhaps also a theologian, who would debate the issue with calm detachment. In the end they would agree that there is no answer to the dilemma of why suffering should exist if God is both good and all powerful. Some suffering can be explained as the result of human evil. Some pain is useful as a warning against greater dangers. But in the end there is still an irreducible remainder of suffering which serves no purpose and has no obvious cause. To many people the extent of suffering and its irrationality is the main obstacle to belief in God. Far better to suppose that the universe came into being by chance or has always existed, material, aimless, and without feeling or caring. Our poet takes one man, tells his story, allows him and his wife and his friends to speak, and if at the end he has no answer to the 'problem of suffering', he has enlarged our understanding of religious devotion.

For the Christian the testing of Job's faith is almost as great a problem as the disasters that afflict him. What kind of a God would so treat his faithful servant? It is a question we have attempted to examine, though without finding any answer. Yet we find it hard to see here the Father of Jesus Christ, even though the sufferings which Christ had to endure were Job's, and his final cry expressed the same sense of being abandoned by God. It may be that we treat the cross too lightly, and the sufferings of men and women down the ages should be linked with our Lord's sufferings more intimately.

We must also listen to the voice of feminists, though Elizabeth Cady Stanton, one of the first to rebel against a society controlled by men, a society which she held was bolstered up by the Bible, hardly sounds like one: [Job's] last affliction was the disgust of his wife. She ridiculed his faith in God, and scoffed at his piety, as Michal did at David. She was spared to be his last tempter when all his comforts were taken away. She bantered him for his constancy, "Dost thou still maintain thy confidence in the God who has punished thee? Why dost thou be so obstinate in thy religion, which serves no good to thee? Why truckle to a God who, so far from rewarding thy services with marks of his favor, seems to take pleasure in making thee miserable and scourges thee without any provocation? Is this a God to be still loved and served? 'Curse God and Die.' " She urges him to commit suicide. Better to die at once than to endure his life of lingering misery.' It is the voice of common sense, and Stanton adds: 'Poor woman, she had scraped lint, nursed him and waited on him to the point of nervous exhaustion – no wonder she was resigned to see him pass to Abraham's bosom.'[1] Should we not rather see the predominant patriarchy of the Old Testament in the fact that Job's wife is depicted as the temptress, and rebel against such a view?[2]

Modern psychology and counselling have made much of 'empathy'. There could hardly be a more telling example than the three friends, who sit beside Job on the ground and share his exclusion from the community. Why then do they fail Job in the end? How is it that sympathy and a desire to bring comfort are not enough?

Before leaving the Prologue it will be well again to recall that our poet, who, we have seen, is an Israelite and writes in Hebrew flavour, presents his characters as foreigners. The problem of suffering is universal. All religions have had to come to terms with it, some indeed have found the heart of their saving message here. Closest to our poet, perhaps, is Gautama, the Buddha, protected by his father from any sight of evil and surrounded by every comfort and delight, whose religious quest began when he saw a decrepit old man, a diseased man, and a corpse. The book of Job releases us from the claustrophobia of a faith too narrowly focused on a chosen people, an elect race, and a single way to God.

And as death levels high and low to the same state, so suffering unites all men and women of every time and people. None has privilege, though in our modern world wealth can buy better hospital care and medical services. A twentieth-century Job would not have found himself on the rubbish heap outside the city. It is only the poor who congregate there.

---

[1] *The Woman's Bible* (1895, 1985 reprint by Polygon Books, pp. 94–95). Few recent feminists pay much attention to Job's wife, most being concerned with 'womb' imagery in the speeches.

[2] The *Testament of Job* written between 100 BC and AD 100, probably in Hellenistic Jewish circles, not only gives a name to Job's wife (Sitis), but depicts her suffering as she cares for Job and even sells her hair to Satan to purchase loaves. She dies a painful death and Job's second family are the children of the second wife, Dinah.

2 *Job's curse and lament*

Christians often feel that they should show the kind of resignation which Job showed in the Prologue.[1] It is good that our poet, like many of the psalmists, realized that a sufferer needs to express his inner feelings, even when they are rebellious or despairing. Job had kept silent with his friends for seven days. Was he struggling with his distress? Silent companionship, as we have seen, can often provide the best comfort, but Job found the silence oppressive. Now he bursts out.

He hides nothing of his pain. Would that he had never been born! Would that he might go down to Sheol, the land of tranquillity and peace! He curses the day of his birth, but he does not curse his God. For a fleeting moment he questions the ordering of life. Why are human beings 'hedged about by God on every side'? Even in his personal distress his thought reaches beyond his own sorrows. He knows that he is not the only one who is suffering. 'Why should this happen to me?' has become, 'Why is life given to those who find it so bitter?'

Job's anguished cries remind the Christian that modern medical practice gives to human beings power over the lives of their fellows that earlier generations did not possess. We can heal diseases that claimed innumerable victims in the past. We can control pain. We have set up hospices for the terminally ill so that they may live out their remaining days surrounded by love and when death comes they may leave this world with dignity.

But we have abandoned the Hippocratic Oath and permit doctors to destroy life as well as to save it – even though there are violent arguments about whether the foetus is a human person as soon as conception takes place, and oppposing pressure groups seek to restrict abortion or to permit abortion on demand. Euthanasia is still a criminal offence in Great Britain, though not in some other countries, but the debate on whether doctors should be permitted to ease the death of a sufferer has begun. And with intensive care and the means to restart a heart that has stopped beating questions arise about when to allow a man or a woman to die.

Longings such as Job expressed have been echoed by many a sufferer in the dark watches of the night. It is the eternal Why? Yet

[1] It is the patience of Job which the author of the Epistle of James singles out (James 5.7–11). The intertestamental *Testament of Job* also stresses Job's patience and has little understanding of his later outbursts.

when we debate abortion and ask whether children who are likely to be born deformed or to suffer from grievous disabilities would not be saved much suffering if they were aborted in the early stages of pregnancy, we also need to listen to the cry of the disabled: 'If all foetuses which were likely to develop deformities had been aborted, I should not be here, and life is precious to me.' We need to weigh up the arguments on either side in the abortion and euthanasia debates and to try to understand what are the latest developments in medicine, but then it is a Christian judgment which we have to make.

Yet has not the Satan won half his wager? 'Skin for skin! To save himself there is nothing a man will withhold' (1.4). It was not until his skin was marked by disease that Job showed any grief or questioning. Nothing in all his speeches would reveal to the reader that his seven sons and three daughters had perished in an hour. And this is not a hiding of sorrow which belongs to a culture different from our own. David's anguished cry, 'O, my son! Absalom my son, my son Absalom! Would that I had died instead of you! O Absalom, my son, my son' (II Sam. 18.33) reaches out to us across the centuries. The pain and loyalty of Rizpah is felt and understood (II Sam. 21.10). Why, even Paltiel shows more emotion than Job (II Sam. 3.15).

The pain of bereavement is real and noble. Autobiography and novel help us to understand both the griefs of others and our own sorrows. E. M. Blaiklock allows us to stand alongside him in his 'unbroken anguish' in *Kathleen: A Record of a Sorrow* (Hodder & Stoughton, 1980). Susan Hill must surely reflect something of her own experiences in her moving novel *In the Springtime of the Year*. Callimachus's ode touches our heart more than the ravings of Job:

> They told me, Heraclitus, they told me you were dead,
> They brought me bitter news to hear and bitter tears to shed.
> I wept as I remember'd, how often you and I
> Had tired the sun with talking and sent him down the sky.
>
> And now that thou art lying, my dear old Carian guest,
> A handful of grey ashes, long, long ago at rest,
> Still are thy pleasant voices, they nightingales, awake;
> For Death, he taketh all away, but them he cannot take.[2]

Job asks his bitter questions, but in this chapter he does not contemplate ending his own life, and only fleetingly blames God for his distress. It is when the friends press the question of theodicy and the

---

[2] William Cory's translation.

connection between sin and suffering that he leaps to the desperate conclusion that he has been rejected by God and that God has become his enemy. The failure of the friends is perhaps the most tragic feature of the whole book. They came with such good intentions. They shared his silent suffering. But when he uttered this curse and bitter lament their response only increased his anguish.

Our poet, writing so long ago, teaches us much about sharing suffering and offering comfort. He also shows how destructive a too confident faith can be.

3   *The failure of the friends*

The friends were true friends. They had made careful arrangements and travelled long distances to console Job. Great was their grief when they found him quite literally changed beyond recognition. They went to where he was and sat in silent sympathy for seven days by his side on the refuse heap outside of the city. It was not for lack of caring or want of compassion that they failed. And yet as soon as the first of them had spoken Job castigates them as dried up wadis, disappointing those who desperately search for water. How could this be?

To discover why we so often fail to comfort one another and why the most devout may be the least able to soothe the bruised heart we have only to look at Eliphaz. Elderly, kindly, courteous, he approaches Job gently and considerately, and acknowledges Job's goodness. His religion is no mere reciting of a creed nor ritual observance. He can draw an attractive picture of the happiness of those who receive God's blessing. If such a man as Eliphaz fails we must surely recognize the difficulty of bringing relief to the one who suffers.

The first reason is that he never fully understood Job's feelings. 'Think how strong you used to be when all was going well. Now as soon as adversity touches you how completely you crumple. Your piety should reassure you. For my part, I would appeal to God' (cf. 4.3–6; 5.8). It is well meant, as our exhortations so often are. We see only the outside of the person and lack the imagination to enter into their heartbreak. We fail to understand that a faith which fitted the good days perfectly will not sustain the days of pain. To remind the sufferer of his glad confidence before the disaster struck can only add to his sufferings by making him aware of the inadequacy of his faith and the insecure foundations upon which he must now rebuild his life. The recollection of past piety is no reassurance in this situation.

The 'If I were in your place' approach is still more devastating. For the sufferer knows that his friends are *not* in his place. Their lack of understanding shows this all too clearly. To shovel out advice from the security of good health and a stable home cannot bring help to the one whose life has fallen in.[1]

Neither will platitudes bring reassurance. It is strange that in moments of the greatest joy or need we fall back on stock phrases. Eliphaz's night vision spoke a disappointing message: 'Can a human being be righteous before God, a mere mortal pure before his Maker?' (4.17). For platitudes do not key into the particular. Proverbial wisdom is moulded from statistical averages. No one likes to be a statistic. No one is willing to be merely a type. For we all know that we are unique, each one of us – even identical twins!

There is a further reason why Eliphaz failed: he placed faith before friendship. It was gently done. The other friends will be more brusque. But whereas Job had uttered his curse and made his lament, it had come from anguish of heart and a broken spirit, not from a sense of injustice or of faith betrayed. Only as he looked away from his own sorrows to the general suffering of humankind did he think fleetingly of the way our lives are hedged in and we are unable to find full enjoyment and satisfaction. Because Eliphaz does not suffer, even his sympathy is detached. When he speaks, it is across a gulf of pity. 'Think how you once encouraged many. . . . Does your piety give you no assurance?' (4.3, 6). And immediately doctrine replaces understanding. It is decked out as experience, but it is doctrine none the less. For like all of us he sees only what fits in with his creed and is blind to the rest. He holds firm to his religion, and his religion is retribution. Even his suggestion that suffering may be a discipline is soon swallowed up in his picture of the way the pious are shielded from all danger. Job is forgotten. How strangely Eliphaz's description of a home where nothing is amiss and descendants are many must have sounded in Job's ears (5.19–26). The last sentence of Eliphaz's speech gives it away. It is not his personal discovery. He sets himself with the wise men. 'We have enquired into all this, and so it is' (5.27).

In the first cycle of speeches the friends at least try to relate their theology to Job by persuading him of its truth. In the second cycle they can only dispute, their sole argument being the fate of the

---

[1] See Job 16.2–5 for Job's reaction.

wicked and the rewards of the just. They end by openly accusing Job of blatant sin. Dogma has taken over.

Bildad refuses to believe that God will 'pervert justice' (8.3). Tradition is more reliable than the knowledge which we can attain in our short lives, and tradition affirms that God 'will not spurn the blameless man' (8.20). Job can be reassured. His sufferings will soon pass.

Zophar is blunter, for he is shocked by Job's irreverent words. He is the first openly to state that Job deserves his punishment, though the other two friends have hinted at it. With supreme confidence that he fully understands God's rule of the world, he urges Job to put away his iniquity. Then he will 'forget trouble' (11.14–19). It is only a man who has had no acquaintance with suffering who can make this easy promise.

By the time he has heard Job's replies to the first round of speeches even Eliphaz is losing patience. Job's words are 'hot-air arguments'. He accuses Job of abandoning all reverence for God. Even if he were blameless at first, his denial of the orthodox faith now merits condemnation. Eliphaz repeats the creed that has been handed down from the ancestors and which he believes he can confirm from experience. Bildad is affronted that Job will not accept their wisdom, and sets out the same account of the fate of the wicked. Zophar is outraged at Job's arguments and repeats the same stock theory. Job's plight is now forgotten. Theory has triumphed.

If the theory is correct – and the friends become more certain of this the longer they argue with Job – then Job must be a sinner. Eliphaz sets out the sins of a powerful sheik (22.6–9). These are Job's sins without a doubt. He should repent. Bildad can only mumble on about the insignificance of human beings and the impossibility that any 'mere mortal' can be 'justified in God's sight' (25.4–6).

Surely, we say, as we read the speeches of the friends, only the Inquisition or strict Calvinists of a past century would treat a sufferer in this way. We live in a kinder age. It is not so.

Martin Camroux's first son was born severely brain damaged due to lack of oxygen in the latter stages of the delivery. He lived for only three days. Martin and his wife discovered that they were surrounded by a great wave of sympathy and support, and found the greatest help from those who did not try to tell them anything except that they cared – like the lady who called and said, 'We don't know what to do', and then handed them a cake. That said it all. Least helpful were those who tried to give religious advice. One lady called, thrust a tract under their noses, and made them sit and read it. One line of comfort they found particularly offensive – that what had happened was God's will. A fellow minister said, 'God does work in strange ways, but next time you pray, "They will be done", I will be there helping you. "The Lord giveth and the Lord taketh away. Blessed be the name of the Lord." '[2]

Again we have to ask, What kind of a God is it who will strike down babies? What God do those really believe in who say that God's will is hard to understand when a mother of two small children is knocked off her bicycle and killed as she cycles to school?

The failure of the friends raises two questions for Christian readers today.

The first we have considered several times already. How do we offer true comfort to the sufferer? The answer which the book of Job gives is that it will not be by our speaking but in our silence. By just being there. By placing the arm round the shoulders, writing the letter when we do not know what to say and admit it, taking a little gift. Explanations and debate are for a later time, not for now. And those who have suffered will tell us that this is so.

But the problem of suffering is there and has to be faced. Although the writer of the book of Job probably did not intend his work to be a theodicy, the suffering which Job endured and the speeches of the friends make it impossible to evade the question of why human beings suffer as they do.

One thing is plain. Whether the writer has an answer to give or not, he is convinced that suffering is not necessarily a punishment for sin. The friends may try to search out some wrongs for which Job is being punished, but they are simply setting up text-book situations and Job does not fit any of them. Job admits that he is not perfect, but he denies that he has committed any wrong that merits such a dreadful punishment as he has received, and in the end God declares him in the right. God's estimate of Job's character is true: 'You will find no one like him on earth, a man of blameless and upright life, who fears God and sets his face against wrongdoing' (1.8). The friends' theology is wrong. Although suffering may sometimes be the result of sin, because a man or a woman suffers it cannot be regarded as proof that they have sinned.

As we read the speeches of the friends we are struck by their self-confidence. They claim to know exactly how God runs the world. Even the cautious and kindly Eliphaz is certain from the first. He has enquired into the matter and knows it to be true. The good man will

---

[2] Martin Camroux, 'Thank God for Mark', *The Expository Times* 99, 1987–88, p. 180.

be protected while 'those who plough mischief and sow trouble reap no other harvest' and 'perish at the blast of God' (4.8–9). Later he describes the 'anxiety' which racks the wicked and the troubles that come upon him, and ends by saying that no one can escape the eye of the all-seeing God, who 'brings down the pride of the haughty and keeps safe those who are humble' (22.29). Tradition, revelation and experience combine to assure him that he possesses the truth. Bildad relies more upon the 'older generations' and their wisdom (8.8) and with utter self-possession sets out the punishments which come upon the evildoer (18.5–21). Zophar is the most surprising, for he combines a keen sense of the transcendent and incomprehensible God with a certainty that he knows exactly how this God governs the universe. He can assert that 'since time began . . . the triumph of a wicked person is short-lived', describe in detail the punishments which befall the wicked, and tell Job, 'God exacts from you less than your sin deserves (cf. 11.7–12; 20.4–29; 11.6). This is a sad feature of the faith of many earnest people. The more confident their faith the more convinced they seem to be that they possess complete insight into the mind of God.

We need to read Camus alongside of Job. In *The Plague* Father Paneloux preaches two sermons. Before he had personally met those who were dying, he proclaimed the orthodox doctrine: 'Calamity has come on you, my brethren, and, my brethren, you deserved it.' During the weeks that follow he works alongside the atheistic Dr Bernard Rieux. One day they sit beside a young boy who is dying in agony. Peneloux gazes down at the small mouth fouled by the sordes of the plague and pouring out the angry death-cry that has sounded through the ages of mankind. He sinks onto his knees: 'My God, spare this child. . .'. The boy dies, and Dr Rieux swings round fiercely to Fr Paneloux: 'That child, anyhow, was innocent – and you know it as well as I do!' The priest replies: 'That sort of thing is revolting because it passes human understanding. But perhaps we should love what we cannot understand.' Dr Rieux straightened up slowly. 'No, Father. I've a very different idea of love. And until my dying day I shall refuse to love a scheme of things in which children are put to torture.' So Father Paneloux climbs into his pulpit to preach his second sermon. This time he no longer addresses the congregation as 'You'. He reminds them of an earlier plague in Marseilles. Only four out of eighty-one monks in Mercy Monastery survived. Of these four, three took to flight. . . . 'My brothers, each one of us must be the one who stays.'

The friends say some true things, and many false ones. Although they speak at length, they do not advance beyond the theology they held at the beginning. They suppose that the more they repeat the dogma they have received, the more secure the dogma will be. It is not for the speeches of the friends that we read the book of Job. We must turn to Job himself.

4 Job speaks

Our poet probably intended his work to be recited. Only by reading the whole book in the order in which it is written can we appreciate its power. But this is a commentary, dull, pedestrian, without inspiration. It probes and dissects, and through its probing and its dissection it kills. We shall examine Job's speeches by topics, snatching a verse here and a passage there to build up a skeleton of his thought and emotions. Those who prefer the living and suffering human being should return to what the poet himself has given to us.

We have looked at Job's first speech already, because it needed this outburst to get the dialogue going. Had he remained silent in his distress, or meekly submitted to God, the friends would have continued to support him and there would have been no debate. The response he gave in the Prologue was what they required. It fitted in with their false theology. But Job did not remain silent. He cursed the day of his birth and complained about his suffering. To his 'Why?' they had to make answer. But how did he react to their words?

(a) Job and the friends

An acute sense of disappointment runs through Job's speeches. He had looked for so much from his friends, and they have failed him. He had made no demands upon them, but they have not even stood by him in his despair and loss of faith in God (6.14–23). They have become 'trouble-makers', treating him as a stubborn windbag, who will not see sense (16.2–3). Their words grieve and crush him (19.2). If he had been in their place he would have offered encouragement – but it is all too easy for those who do not have to endure torment to harangue the one who suffers (16.4–5). To the end they bring no help to the one bereft of strength (26.2–3). They have insulted him with their false accusations. As if it were not enough that God has become his enemy, they emulate God and pursue him too (19.3–5, 22). And he cries out to them in his anguish, 'Pity me, have pity on me, you that are my friends' (19.21).

We have already seen that the friends failed Job because they placed theology before friendship. That is our cold way of expressing it when we try to maintain an academic objectivity. To Job it feels very different. If they cannot bring comfort, why will they not be silent (13.5, cf. v. 13)? The words of the upright are harsh indeed, hitting a man when he is down (6.25, 27). For their arguments are false. He had asked them to show him what sin he had committed that brought this punishment upon him (6.24) and they had complied! They not only condemned his frenzied speech, they listed the sins he must have committed. Job is outraged. The one certainty upon which he stakes his all is his integrity (6.29). He will not allow them to be in the right:

> Far be it from me to concede that you are right!
> Till I cease to be, I shall not abandon my claim to innocence.
> I maintain and shall never give up the rightness of my cause;
> so long as I live, I shall not change (27.5).

They 'go on smearing truth with [their] falsehoods' and stitch 'a patchwork of lies' (13.4). Believing that they are defending God, their speech is 'wicked' (13.7). They had pointed to the misfortunes which had befallen him and had judged him a grievous sinner – but God will be the judge (19.27c–29). Their theology is wholly false. He has as much experience as they have, and he knows that there are evil men who prosper and good men who are overwhelmed with disasters (12.2–3; 13.1–2; 21.7–33). Their answers are totally wrong (21.34). Twice Job ignores the friends as he pours out his soul in a monologue and in prayer to this strange God who rules the world so unjustly and remains silently aloof from humankind (chs. 9–10 and 23–24). From the friends who possess so little understanding of his plight and view the world in such a biased way Job can only turn away, defending his integrity before God, though it cost him his life (13.13–20).

The book of Job has much to offer to pastoral counsellors. When should we speak and when be silent? How can we bridge the gulf between the outsider who cannot suffer as the client suffers and the client in his despair? What dangers are there in thinking that our training has given insight into the psyche of the client? In these days it is unlikely that social workers will hold so firmly to a theology that it affects their relations with their clients, but may not psychology have taken its place? We speak today of the 'management' of grief, and offer counselling in those whose hearts are broken. Thinking to be kind, a doctor gave tranquillizers to a daughter whose parents had been killed. Her minister said he had heard nothing so fearful as her uncontrollable laughter at the graveside. Do we not need to think things out afresh?

Here is the great difference between Job and the friends. He speaks out of experience: they strive to fit his life into a too rigid theology. This is why their arguments do not change throughout the debate. The only advance is that their words become more shrill.

(b) Job and his God

Job's attitude to the friends is consistent, for he realizes as soon as Eliphaz has spoken that they have no inkling of his condition. Their theology is false. They will not admit that they may be wrong. They are determined to fit him into the mould which they have made. His own relations with God are vastly different. It will be best to trace once more Job's prayers and criticisms as our poet has set them out.

Unlike Christians in the present century, the option of setting buffers between God and the world was not open to Job. He would not have been willing to accept it, even if it had been. God is in control. He must take the blame for everything that happens in his universe. The responsibility is his.

So in his first reply to Eliphaz Job can say:

> The arrows of the Almighty find their mark in me,
> and their poison soaks into my spirit;
> God's onslaughts wear me down (6.4).

Again in that first speech we find that most striking feature that marks Job off from the friends – he prays to God. 'Sound' theology is not religion. The friends exert their strenuous efforts to defend God's justice, and they can counsel Job to submit and confess his sin, but it never occurs to them to pray themselves. Job, even though he can describe God as a tyrant, a torturer, a celestial spy, cannot hold back from offering prayer.

A second feature is more curious. Job never addresses God by his name.[1] Often he does not even use one or other of the general words

---

[1] 12.9 is such an astonishing exception that it is surprising that REB did not follow most commentators and regard it as a textual error. It may be that our poet did not allow the characters to use the name Yahweh because they are depicted as non-Israelites. He could retain the name in the narratives and the introductions to the speeches, for he was a Jew. Another suggestion is that the line is a reminiscence of Isa. 41.20c.

for God that our poet employs. In this first speech we should not know that he had begun to pray at 7.7 were not the singular verbs pointed out to us. At several points REB inserts 'God' to make it plain that the talk is about God or to him.

We recall that he has just pictured God as an archer, directing his arrows at him, yet too much of a sadist to kill him outright and give him relief from his anguish. Now he pleads with this malevolent deity. His life is 'but a breath of wind'. Those who go down to Sheol are like a cloud that breaks up and disperses. So fragile a creature, so fleeting his existence, yet God treats him as if he were one of the chaos monsters. He terrifies him with nightmares. The loving care of which the Psalmist sang has turned into a spiteful surveillance. God is ever on the lookout for his least slip. And yet Job prays – and says all this in his prayer!

Who of us would dare to pray like this? Many of the psalms have been censored or bowdlerized when used in public worship. It is an anaemic faith that we proclaim. Our plea would no doubt be that we have not so learnt Christ. God is now Abba – and with a sentimentality which most certainly is alien to the world of Jesus, we have made God a daddy and our address to Christ is 'Dear Lord, we just want to say . . .'. Job's honesty is surely more to the liking of God than the way we hide our true feelings. Some of the prayers of Michel Quoist contain such an honesty despite their affectation.

So Job comes to his final plea.

> Why do you not pardon my offence
> and take away my guilt?
> For soon I shall lie in the dust of the grave;
> you may seek me, but I shall be no more.

Has he given everything away with these final words? Perhaps. None of us is totally consistent. He may have had a passing doubt about his innocence. Christians, unlike the ancient Israelites, have put sin at the centre of their religion, for it makes the atonement necessary. We are uneasy every time Job asserts that he is blameless. This prayer fits our ears more happily. But perhaps the words are ironic. 'Why will not God forgive the sin which he falsely believes I have committed if that will satisfy him?' The emphasis, however, is on the last two lines. He cannot believe that God really wishes to cast off his faithful servant. Yet if he does not act soon it will be too late. God may 'seek him diligently' as the older translations rendered the verb, but he will be no more. We shall have to face the annihilation of Sheol later.

As we have seen, after the speech of Bildad Job cannot bring himself to speak directly to the friends. He describes what the world looks like to him and then returns to prayer. God is all powerful. No one can win a law-suit against him, for he will not answer any questions. His might is seen in nature, but he himself is a hidden God. No one can challenge him. He will not accept that Job is blameless. Worse, he is heedless of right and wrong, and 'mocks the plight of the innocent'. It is he who has put wicked men in control of human affairs; he it is who blindfolds the judges so that they cannot discern between innocent and guilty. It is a grim account.

And it gets worse. Job is convinced that God will never acquit him. Even if he attempted to wash himself clean, God would thrust him back into the mire – no, not God: '*you*, says Job, 'would thrust me into the miry pit' (9.31). From being heedless of right and wrong God has become the one who delights in suffering, who refuses to allow Job to rid himself of sin. But it is at this darkest, harshest point that Job forgets that he is talking about God and addresses him directly.

I suppose it was the Lisbon earthquake on 1 November 1755 which put an end to the popular religious view that earthquakes were directly sent by God to punish sinners. For it was All Saints' Day. The churches were full. Thousands were killed, particularly those at worship. We today distinguish between disasters which occur because that is the nature of the physical world, and wrongs committed by sinful men and women. But along the way God has been edged out of his world. Ours is no longer a God who 'moves mountains before they know it' and shakes the 'pillars' of the earth. We do not readily suppose that God either blindfolds the eyes of judges or gives them the intelligence to come to a true judgment. The God of the late twentieth century is more elusive than Job's God, even though he could not see him when he went by. We shall have to consider how we can 'think magnificently about God'[2] when we come to the speeches by Yahweh. For the moment we will accept that Job's picture of the all powerful and immoral God is alien to our ways of thinking. Yet it expresses two important features that must not be passed by. In the ultimate God is responsible for the physical evil in the world, for it was this world that he created and none other. Any attempt we make to find an answer to the problem of evil will be inadequate if it does not face up to this. And secondly, Job does not abandon his faith to God. This is what the world looks like to him. Yet he still turns to prayer.

---

[2] The heading of one of the chapters in A. J. Gossip's wonderful book on prayer, *In the Secret Place of the Most High*, Independent Press 1946, Scribners 1947.

'If only . . .' God is too powerful to challenge. If only there were a mediator greater than God himself, able to 'impose his authority' on both God and his servant. There is no mediator, and Job determines to speak directly to God setting out what he will say. It is an audacious speech, defiant in its honesty.

And then, yet again, from thinking out what he would say if he could approach God, Job finds himself praying to this strange deity. He had said that none could save him from God's hand, and suddenly realizes that it was those hands that created him. With a prayer akin to Ps. 139 he gives thanks for God's providence – only to spring a bitter twist at the end. Such apparent love: such a demonic plan. The divine watcher, the sacred assailant. Why? Better to have died at birth. Again there is the spectre of Sheol, the 'land of dense darkness and disorder', no longer the place where the weary and oppressed find rest, as in ch. 3.

To the Christian the mention of a mediator immediately awakens the thought of *the* Mediator. But how different this Mediator is! Not the one with power even over God, but the one who came in the form of a servant and died as only rebellious slaves and terrorists did. And though the sufferer still asks his insistent 'Why?', he is no longer alone. The Son also uttered his 'Why?' And at the end of this life there is no longer the gloom of Sheol, even if there is no return to this world.

Has this prayer of Job meaning any longer, then? Meaning for Christians, who have the resurrection assurance; meaning for those who do not believe in God's existence, for whom there is no super-human power, God or devil, to torture humankind. Faith and unfaith seem to disallow it. Always, however, as we read Job we are arrested by the 'And yet. . .'. There are times when the New Testament is too confident, too free from doubt and suffering for our modern world. The evils are too massive for an easy way of salvation. To us Mark's account of the crucifixion is more congenial than Luke's or John's, and the silence at the end of Mark's whole gospel sometimes carries more meaning than the idyllic Emmaus Road or the breakfast by the lakeside. Even the most confident Christian must sometimes wonder what lies beyond as he stands by an open grave. The Christian faith may give the theological answer: that answer is not always the answer which harmonizes with the Christian's doubts and fears. When the insistent 'Why?' cannot be silenced it may help to remember that, although Job saw only God the torturer and the silence of the land of no return, he did two things: he refused to renounce his integrity and he would not abandon prayer.

Mary Craig's second baby suffered from Höhler's Syndrome – gargoylism. She struggled on in the face of thoughtless doctors. She looked after him at home even though an old family friend passed them in the street without a word, and coming to the house next day almost shouted at her, 'An animal, that's what he is, an animal. Why don't you have him put away?' The turning point in her despair came one day on holiday. She could not relax. Her rather vague religion had deserted her. Self-pity came surging as a tide. One evening she found herself alone in an empty church. She muttered a defiant if muddled, 'Damn you, you don't exist, but I hate you.' Then, bursting into tears, she threw decorum to the winds and found herself shouting, 'All right, if you do exist show me a way out. For a start, what the hell am I to do next?' Then, startled at the noise she was making, she ran out of the church and back to her husband and family in their holiday home. That night she read a book about the Sue Ryder Home for Concentration Camp Victims in Cavendish, and went to help for a week. It ended happily, with renewed faith and renewed ability to help others, but after a long slog.[3] The need to be honest with oneself and to talk honestly to God is perhaps the most pressing – and healing – of all.

When Job next speaks of God his mood is little lighter. He knows he is 'innocent and blameless' and has prayed to God, yet God has afflicted him, though evil men are 'left undisturbed' (12.4–6). His hymn of praise looks only at the destructive wonders that God works: again we ask, 'Is this a God or a demon?' (12.13–25). And yet again the wonder is that although Job says that he has seen all this with his own eyes, nevertheless he is still eager to speak to God, still ready to argue with him (13.3). He will defend himself even if God kills him (13.14–16), for, strange as it may seem, he cannot doubt that if only he could get through to God and state his case he would be acquitted (13.18).

So once more he prays – without introduction, without formal opening: 'Grant me these two conditions.' Who is in charge at the opening of this law-suit? It is Job who tells God that he leaves the choice to him. He may summon and question him, or he will himself present the case for God to answer. What is his crime? Why is he treated as an enemy? Why does God drag up all the minor misdemeanours of his youth? How cruel to harass one as shortlived as a human being, who has no hope after death. Job takes the initiative here. And then wistfully he expresses the longings of his

---

[3] Mary Craig, *Blessings*, Hodder & Stoughton and Morrow 1979.

soul. If only God would hide him away until his anger had subsided! Surely God does love this creature he has made. It is a passing dream. In reality God has stored up every offence and will destroy him as he destroys all human beings. Even a man's slaves care more for their master than God does for his faithful worshipper (13.20–14.22).

It is an awesome indictment and comes within the width of a four-letter word to the curse which the Satan had predicted. Some say that by the end of this speech God had lost his wager. The silent God, the mocking God, the unjust God, the divine spy, the celestial persecutor, the one who uses his naked and brutal power to crush weak mortals and to turn his creation back to chaos – how much closer could Job get to fulfilling the Satan's prediction?

And yet . . . Job still prays, still wants to meet this strange and terrible God.

This is the place where a white, male, middle-class, Western college lecturer can write no more. The black South African, the Latin American peasant, women raped, oppressed, humiliated, crushed by the burden of work in every country of the world are the ones who can understand. Let a Liberation Theologian speak in his place:

It is not possible to do theology in Latin America without taking into account the situation of the most downtrodden of history; this means in turn that at some point the theologian must cry out, as Jesus did, 'My God, my God, why hast thou forsaken me?' . . . How can we talk about God without referring to our own age? More than that: How can we do it without taking into account situations like the holocaust in which God seems to be absent from immense human suffering?

It needs to be realized, however, that for us Latin Americans the question is not precisely, 'How are we to do theology after Auschwitz?' The reason is that in Latin America we are still experiencing every day the violation of human rights, murder, and the torture that we find so blameworthy in the Jewish holocaust of World War II. Our task here is to find the words with which to talk about God in the mist of the starvation of millions, the humiliation of races regarded as inferior, discrimination against women, especially women who are poor, systematic social injustice, a persistent high rate of infant mortality, those who simply 'disappear' or are deprived of their freedom, the sufferings of peoples who are struggling for their right to live, the exiles and the refugees, terrorism of every kind, and the corpse-filled common graves of *Ayacucho* ['the corner of the dead']. What we must deal with is not the past but, unfortunately, a cruel present and a dark tunnel with no apparent end.

Gutiérrez says that we cannot keep silent in the midst of such contempt for human life, and quotes St Gregory the Great: 'the cry of Jesus will not be heard "if our tongues keep silent about what our souls believe. But lest his cry be stifled in us, let each of us make known to those who approach him the mystery by which he lives." '[4]

When Job next speaks it is still of this same inhuman God who has 'left [him] at the mercy of malefactors', savaged him, 'set [him] up as his target', rushed on him like a warrior (16.11–14). Yet he will not abandon his plea of innocence or check his cry for justice. If only there were an arbitrator – but since there is not he must appeal to God against this monstrous God. We noted the marvellous way in which our poet in this speech in chs. 16–17 has portrayed the vehement passion of this sufferer who will not submit to his fate or bow down before an unjust God. Here as we seek to interpret the religious meaning of his words we set side by side the griefs he enumerates: friends who are 'trouble-makers' and 'gloat' as they see his sufferings and gnash at him with their teeth, a God who treats him so cruelly, his own distress and pain, and at the end only Sheol where hope has to be abandoned, for there will be no one to take account of his piety. And still he prays!

Gutiérrez quotes Miguel de Unamuno:

> I want to see you, Lord, and then die,
> die wholly;
> but to see you, Lord, to see your face,
> to know who you are!
> Look at me with your eyes,
> those scorching eyes,
> look at me and let me see you!
> Let me see you, Lord, and then die![5]

This Methodist commentator was reminded of Charles Wesley's verse, though it is based upon different biblical passages:

> I cannot see Thy face, and live,
>   Then let me see Thy face, and die!
> Now, Lord, my gasping spirit receive;
>   Give me on eagle's wings to fly,

---

[4] Gustavo Gutiérrez, *On Job*, pp. 101–3. See the account of Gutiérrez's understanding of the book below, pp. 136f.
[5] Ibid., p. 125

> With eagle's eyes on Thee to gaze,
> And plunge into the glorious blaze!

Job's cry for justice becomes more insistent in ch. 19. God himself has 'put him in the wrong'. When he cries out there is no answer: when he makes his appeal he gets no justice (19.6–7). God has fenced him in, stripped him of all honour, treated him as an enemy (19.8–11). He is alone. Relations and friends keep aloof, his slave-girls treat him as a stranger, his wife will not come near, his loved ones have turned against him. The three friends press their charges with the same ruthlessness that God has shown. And the finality of death is near. At this darkest moment, when the only hope of vindication appears to be an inscription which records for those who come after the innocence of this man who was falsely condemned, Job makes his great leap of faith. God will vindicate him – and he will see it.

The all too Christian confidence of Handel's aria is now seen to be an interpretation which the Hebrew cannot sustain. In any case the text is so obscure and corrupt that no translation can be certain. We may as well stick with REB as any other. Yet if we stay with it we shall still stand before a hope that can only humble us. Job cannot abandon the Sheol belief. Death he knows is the end. His only confidence lies in his refusal to admit that he has committed any wrong deserving of so great a punishment. The friends desire that he should deny himself in order to secure ease from his suffering and the restoration of his fortunes. This he will not do. And he cannot believe that God, tyrant though he is, would wish him to.

So the Satan has not won his wager after all. For Job will not grovel before God in order to secure a comfortable life.

What more is there for Job to say? In his next speech he looks away from himself to the injustices of the world (ch. 21). In chs. 23–24 he reiterates his confidence in his innocence and reaffirms his belief that if he could only get through to God he would be able to convince him that he had made a ghastly mistake. And from the disorder of his final speech we can sift out his refusal to abandon his certainty that his cause is just. It only remains for him to survey his life and enter his final plea.

Throughout the book of Job the Sheol belief underlies the argument. Job may make occasional forays into a richer hope, but they are only longings. He knows that death is the end and if he is to be justified it must be in this world. The 'if only' is full of intense longing, but Job knows that it is unattainable. No one can be hidden in Sheol and then brought back to enjoy God's friendship after his anger has passed. He may glimpse his vindication, but in the end he will languish in Sheol, justice satisfied but hope unrealized. The dark shadow of the land of no return covers the whole book.

There was a time when Christians would have countered this with a confidence in the immortality of the soul. There was a time when the resurrection faith was triumphant. Pains were willingly accepted because there was the vital belief that after a brief sojourn in this vale of tears there stretched out an eternity of bliss. It is no longer so. The spirit of a secular age has entered into the Christian church. Incomprehensible is the eager willingness of the young men in Iran to go to their death in the conflict with Iraq with only the promise of heaven as a reward for taking part in the holy war. The philosophical arguments for the immortality of the soul have lost their force. To separate between soul and body seems impossible: how can the mind be parted from the brain? The accounts of the resurrection in the gospels have been shown to be the statements of faith rather than historical records of a dead man brought back to life. The attempts by even the most conservative of Christians to prolong their lives through the advances of modern medicine show that faith in a life after death, however strongly affirmed, is no longer the medieval certainty.

The book of Job speaks to our age in a way that much of the New Testament fails to do. We see a world handed over to the powerful. We mark the oppression of the poor. We hear the cries for justice that receive no answer. And the shadow of a final extinction lies over our world as it does over the book of Job.

Many Christians find the answer of the cross entirely satisfying. The world may seem to be the kind of world that Job said it was, but Jesus has lived. God has entered into this world where injustice reigns, and has allowed himself to be unjustly put to death. And through the appearances of the risen Christ the first disciples were convinced that that cross marked not the triumph of evil but the victory of goodness. The God whom Jesus could address as Father is in control. Job belongs to the Old Testament after all.

Others are not so sure. Life does not seem to make sense. The cross is a more certain fact than the resurrection. 'My God, my God, why have you abandoned me?' sounds truer to experience than 'Today you shall be with me in paradise.' At best God is a silent deity. At worst he may not exist after all. To them the claim that God will provide a parking meter in a busy city for those who have sufficient faith is worse than a trivializing of religion, when God did not lift a finger to prevent six million Jews being killed. The faith of Job is surely more fitted to our condition.

5   *Where can wisdom be found?*

Job and the friends have argued themselves to a standstill. The friends remain confident that they know exactly how God runs the world. Job has become more and more frustrated. He refuses to abandon his confidence in his own integrity and has made his impassioned appeals to God. Now an unnamed bystander speaks. 'Wait', he says. 'Look at the world. Take time to ponder. Where can true wisdom be found?'

We might have expected a biblical writer to be opposed to technology. Surely his message would be that we should rely on God and accept the world as God made it. But no. Our poet begins his poem with an account of human achievements in mining for metal ore and precious stones. He depicts the galleries that are cut out, the way the rocks are pierced, the men working in darkness, hanging precariously on ropes, the diverting of streams away from the mines.

It is primitive technology, of course. But there has been a great interest in recent years in industrial archaeology. In this country we are amazed at the way Stone Age man discovered high quality flints and mined them in Norfolk. And the later inventions and manufacturing techniques that we call the industrial revolution are now preserved in museums and open air sites. The ability of human beings to master their environment is impressive and fascinating.

Today we are not so sure that technology is good. Hiroshima, Bhopal, Chernobyl are names engraved in the annals of human disaster. Dust bowls, water pollution, the destruction of the ozone layer, heedless use of fertilizers and pesticides, even the building of offices and roads have soured the new age of human domination of our planet, which now seems so fragile and defenceless. We could not have our way of life without technology. Yet who would go back to a life without aspirins and anaesthetics?

Our poet wonders at man's ingenuity, but he says that that is not true wisdom. Technology will not enable human beings to understand the universe. There is a deeper, truer wisdom.

And our poet says that we shall never discover it. You cannot buy it. You cannot find it anywhere in nature. It cannot be discovered even in the primeval deep or the land of the dead. God alone understands that wisdom.

At this point we might have expected our poet to say, 'And God has revealed it.' But no. this poem is written by one of the agnostics of the Old Testament. Rather like Qoheleth with his, 'Who knows?' Our poet accepts that the secrets of the universe are hidden for ever from mortals.

It is an important point, even though we shall have to consider it again when we come to the divine speeches. For while agnosticism may be the way of the cynic, it lies also at the heart of religious devotion. God is always greater than we can ever understand. We cannot search out his ways or fathom his wisdom. This was the great failure of the friends. Although they trotted out the correct theology about the mystery of the omnipotent God, they believed that they knew exactly how he ran the world. It was also the failure of Job, for he thought that he knew how God should have run the world, and he wanted to tell God that he was not making a very good job of it. Our poet says: God is greater than your thought.

But this is still not all. There is that final verse which some scholars wish to delete as the addition of a later scribe who could not accept the way the mystics have trod. Perhaps it is, but it may not be so.

> The fear of the Lord is wisdom,
> and to turn from evil, that is understanding!

It is so simple: worship and goodness, reverence and love.

So we continue our research to discover a better technology – though it will not make us wise. We need not worry about our doubts about God and his ways, for he is unsearchable. The way for men and women is to bow down in worship and seek goodness and love.

> Beyond the mist and doubt
> Of this uncertain day,
> I trust in thine eternal name,
> Beyond all changes still the same,
> And in that name I pray.
>
> Our restless intellect
> Has all things in its shade,
> But still to thee my spirit clings,
> Serene beyond all shaken things,
> And I am not afraid.

> Still in humility
> We know thee by thy grace,
> For science's remotest probe
> Feels but the fringes of thy robe:
> Love looks upon thy face.[1]

6   Job's life story and final plea

Chapters 29–31 are a microcosm of the whole book. In a poetic narrative that corresponds to Job's initial curse and lament, our poet traces out his former happiness, his present distress, and his final appeal to God. We have already considered these chapters carefully and we need not go over them again. Instead we shall consider their significance for today's readers.

First it is clear that Job accepts the theology of the friends. Goodness should be rewarded, and it *was* rewarded in those days before the disasters struck. The picture is of a wealthy member of society in an Israelite town – powerful, benign, and held in high honour. His goodness was recognized by all. And he had confidence that that goodness would lead to a long life of contentment.

Because our poet shows the theology to be false, both by the scene in heaven and through the debate, it is natural to regard Job's assurance as a false confidence. Yet how deeply it is embedded in our most fundamental attitudes. We expect to reap some reward for our own goodness. We feel that this is how the world should be run. Tragedy has its appeal because it cuts across this conviction, though even there it is often some flaw in the character of the hero which draws the disaster upon him: Lear's inability to judge the devotion of his daughters, Hamlet's indecision, Othello's loving 'not wisely but too well'. Honest would be the man or woman who could affirm that they did not expect to enjoy long life and happiness if they kept from crime and cared for those 'less fortunate than themselves'. Strange though, when the symbol of our faith is a Roman gibbet on which the man whom we claim to be sinless died in agony. And yet perhaps not so strange, for our common morality is based upon it.

It is as he contemplates the distress of the present that Job awakens to religious sensitivity. For as he describes his terrors and says that

[1] Donald Hughes, *Hymns and Songs*, Methodist Publishing House, 1969, No. 6.

115

God 'flung him down in the mud' (30.19) he turns, willingly or unwillingly, to prayer. We have considered this feature of Job's character in the previous section (pp. 104–13) and need not go over the ground again. This short prayer has all the marks of those longer appeals. The God who remains aloof and gives no answer to his pleading, who hands him over to death only after he has tortured him, is the demonic God whom Job has depicted many times.

Job's confidence in his innocence we have seen before. All through the dialogue Job has affirmed that he has never committed any sin that could merit so harsh a penalty. Here we must face up to the charge that Job's is a religion of good works, that he is the Pharisee of the parable (Luke 18.10–14). 'If we say that we have no sin we deceive ourselves and there is no health in us' (I John 1.8) has been taken into the liturgy that has moulded our thinking and our believing. The traditional Christian faith has been founded on the Fall: 'It was through one man that sin entered the world, and through sin death, and thus death pervaded the whole human race, inasmuch as all have sinned' (Rom. 5.12). So it required the obedient sacrifice of the Son to redeem all humankind. In the book of Job our poet made it certain beyond ambiguity or cynical mistrust that Job was indeed innocent.

We shall consider in a later chapter the form of religion which our poet proclaims. Here we ask the question, even granted that we live in a century which has seen such massive evil as the destruction of six million Jews, wars that ravaged Europe and much of the Far East, starvation facing countless thousands in the Third World, violence that makes women and old people afraid and causes mothers to keep their children constantly by their side, does the emphasis which Christianity places upon sin distort our vision of the forms of evil that exist in today's world and the goodness that still survives? We are conscious as no earlier generation has been that sin is not just a matter of the individual committing an evil deed, that sin is built into the structures of society, so that men and women do wrong without knowing it and fail to do right because they have not seen the possibility of the virtuous deed, and the poor are oppressed more because the economy and the social structures are built that way than through the wickedness of evil men and women. Theologians strive to grapple with the changes in theology that this awareness demands. But should we not also listen to the Old Testament which says that goodness is possible, and seeks to live that way of righteousness?

Yet even as we ponder the possibilities of goodness, we have to face the wrongs of which Job was unaware because of the society in which he lived. The most striking feature of the society which Job's great oath of clearance sets before us is the subjugation of women, who had no rights and were under the control of fathers and husbands. And the punishment which Job calls down upon himself should he commit adultery with the wife of a fellow-citizen is that his own wife should become the slave of another man and that she should be raped by other men.

It was a society in which slaves are kept, though the law attempted to ameliorate their condition. It was a society in which widows and the fatherless were likely to be oppressed because they had no one to protect them. It was a society without social security, where the traveller would have to spend the night in the street if no one gave him hospitality, and where the poor had to rely upon the alms of the rich. It was a society in which the wealthy and powerful man could win his case in the law court because the other elders would side with him. Perhaps the fact that Job resisted most of the temptations of this society makes his goodness the more impressive.

The book of Job is even less a book of ethics than it is a theodicy, but these are questions which a reading from our perspective raises and they cannot be passed by.

In many ways Job 31 sets before us an ethic which is akin to the Sermon on the Mount. In others it belongs to its time – as indeed does Jesus's Sermon. We cannot apply the biblical ethic directly to our own society.

The climax of the chapter comes as Job challenges God.

> Let the Almighty state his case against me!
> If my accuser had written out his indictment,
> I should not keep silence and remain indoors.
> No! I should flaunt it on my shoulder
> and wear it like a crown on my head;
> I should plead the whole record of my life
> and present that in court as my defence (31.35–37).

Here we discover the religious meaning of the book. But first we have to listen to the furious Elihu.

7   Elihu

We have seen that Elihu has had a bad time with commentators. True, there were a few who thought that he spoke the considered message of the writer of Job. In their view our poet planned a theodicy, and his answer to the problem of suffering was that it is a discipline. Most, however, either eliminate him altogether as the inartistic addition of an inferior writer, or think that our poet intended him to be treated with derision. When we examined his speeches we concluded that we do not know enough about contemporary taste to decide what our poet had in mind. To us he appears a caricature of the self-confident believer, but our poet and his audience may have seen things differently.

On this common view, much of what Elihu says had previously been put forward by the friends, although with differences in emphasis. He lays greater stress on suffering as a discipline, and expresses the idea in a different way from Eliphaz, for while Eliphaz thought of it as a discipline for past sins, Elihu saw suffering as a warning to the righteous man against future wrong-doing (33.16–30; 36.9–12). He shows less sympathy for Job. He is certain of the truth of his theology, and his conception of the majesty of God means that he does not expect him to come into the human arena, and thinks that it would be beneath the dignity of the omnipotent deity to do so. Like the friends he is affronted at Job's repeated assertions of his innocence and the way he impugns the justice of God. The brashness of this young man repels. His lack of sympathy for Job loses him our respect.

The friends fail to give any help to Job. Elihu does not even try. He is concerned only with argument. Here, then, is the contrast between those who begin with a theology and fit events into it, and Job who originally held the same theology as the friends but will not be false to his experience. No approaches could be more opposed, and it is no wonder that Elihu speaks as brusquely as he does, his repeated references to his youth and his deference to his elders being part of our poet's ironic portrait of the self-confident and angry defender of God's character.

So far we have been following the general line of most commentators. On this interpretation Elihu is an intrusion. We want to hasten to the appearance of God and are impatient at the delay.

Perhaps we should not dismiss him too quickly. It is possible to interpret Elihu's character differently and to see his intervention as essential if Job is to respond rightly to God when he does speak to him.[1]

Suppose our poet does not see Elihu as an object of ridicule. Suppose he intends us to be impressed by his youth and vitality. Suppose we are to admire the way in which the failure of the friends to establish God's justice arouses his anger because he is so concerned for God's good name. Suppose we accept Elihu's claim that he speaks in deference to no one apart from God. Suppose we recognize a genuine devotion to God in this young man. Suppose there is significance in his name, which is the only Hebrew name in the book and which means 'My God is He', perhaps pointing to the central place devotion to God and adoration have in his life. Suppose our poet has deliberately given Elihu a personality, far more vivid than the bland portraiture of the three friends. How then should his intervention be interpreted?

It might mean that Elihu's place in the book is to reveal to Job a fresh understanding of God, so different from the cruel tyrant that Job had imagined him to be. He begins by showing that no one can force God to intervene, yet God is not unconcerned about human activities. Goodness and evil do matter to him. He uses suffering to teach humility and obedience.

So far he has presented well-rehearsed arguments, though with a greater stress on the activity of God than the friends have often shown. But then come the descriptions of God's working in nature that commentators have often despised as poor imitations of the Yahweh speeches. Suppose that Elihu is genuinely on fire with enthusiasm for God and filled with visionary zeal. His speeches will now be seen as psalm-like, directing the worshipper from the creator's works to adoration of the creator himself. The mood is one of wonder and praise.

Suppose that Job has listened to Elihu, rapt and hushed, no longer anxious to marshall arguments in reply. When Elihu falls silent all is ready for the appearance of God, for he has just spoken of God's coming in the storm. 'As Job listens to Elihu, he finds himself being drawn up in mind and spirit into the very life with which this dramatic image pulsates and presently discovers that he is no longer listening to Elihu, but to the voice that speaks out of the storm, the voice of God himself.' Job's suffering are forgotten as he contemplates the majesty and mystery of God. He is ready to respond, and the book

[1] For this interpretation I am indebted to J. W. McKay: 'Elihu – A Proto-Charismatic?', *The Expository Times* 90, 1978–79, pp. 167–171.

119

culminates in his cry, 'I knew of you then only by report, but now I see you with my own eyes', eyes that had been first opened by Elihu.

It may not be so. We can never know. But if it is, then we can see Elihu as a young man filled with religious fervour. To old men he is brash and filled with his own self-importance. Yet his very enthusiasm is what Job needs – someone with a living faith, someone to whom God is the high and lofty one, to be worshipped in awe and reverence, to be known. It will be the response which Job himself will make once has has seen God for himself.

Elihu may make those of us in the church today alert to the value of the exuberance of youth within our worship and Christian service. We need the newly converted, with all their joy in their intimacy with their Lord, even though it may seem to us lacking in depth and failing to sense the incomprehensibility of God. Their theology may be naïve, their certainties slightly absurd, their lack of sympathy towards those with a quieter and less extroverted faith unlovely. Yet if this interpretation of Elihu is right, he was the first to bring healing to Job.

8 Yahweh's speeches and Job's submissions

At last God speaks. As we listen to what he says it becomes clear that whatever may have been the purpose of our poet it was not to solve the mystery of suffering. You cannot introduce God and then make him utter irrelevancies unless you wish to scoff at religion. What God says has to be taken with all seriousness – and it provides no answer to Job's questions. He makes no mention of the wager in heaven. He appears to round on Job. He displays his majestic power, just as Job had said he would, and Job is crushed by it as he had expected. Why, then, does Job say at the end that he is satisfied?

The answer lies in the plot of the drama.[1] Job had refused to be brow-beaten by the friends into making a confession of guilt which he did not feel, naming sins which he knew he had not committed. His faith was in ruins after all the disasters he had suffered, and there were few handholds left that he could grasp. Like the friends he had

[1] The use of this phrase does not imply that I think Job was ever acted or has any relation to drama as normally understood, whether ritual or tragic. It simply points to the fact that there is movement and development of character and ideas in the book – there is a 'story-line'.

believed in an equal apportioning of rewards and punishments according to each man's character and conduct. In his case he knew that it was not so. He was confronted, not with an intellectual riddle, but with a soul-shattering experience. And he had won God's wager for him. He had not denied the experience which was his, and he had not cursed God to his face.

By holding to the one thing of which he could be certain, however, he had still not arrived at a true understanding of religion. Of his innocence he was sure. Of the justice of God he was in doubt. For God seemed to have misjudged his faithful servant, become his enemy, and now was waiting to pass the final sentence before condemning him to the silence of Sheol. Well, he would hold fast to his innocence. He would challenge God. He would demand a verdict.

His actions showed that he still held that theology which the friends had declared with monotonous repetition. The wicked are punished. The righteous are rewarded. God's treatment of him was unjust. Only an acquittal that he could wear as a crown would satisfy him.

It was after God appeared in all his majestic power and showed to Job that he knew nothing of the workings of the mysterious universe which he had created, that Job came to the realization that no one, not even the best of men, not even the man whom God himself declared blameless and upright, could stride into God's presence and claim his rights. Some see this as near to what St Paul meant by justification by faith. Whether this is right or not, it is not to be doubted that our poet has displayed before us the essence of true religion.

For the twentieth-century Christian questions remain.

God had paraded before Job the wonders of nature which he could not understand. It was before these mysteries that Job is humbled and discovered the heart of religion – that the only response to an awareness of the greatness of God is reverence and awe.

But *we* know. We live in a world of scientific discovery and technological achievement.

'Where were you when I laid the earth's foundations?' We were not there but we can reach back to the first few millionths of a second after the 'big bang'.

'Have you visited the storehouses of the snow?' Yes, and we can watch the moving weather systems from a satellite and predict when sunshine and storm will occur.

'Did you proclaim the rules that govern the heavens, or determine the laws of nature on the earth?' No, we did not design those rules but we have searched them out and our mathematical symbols can write them down.

'Do you know when the mountain goats give birth? . . . Can you count the months that they carry their young?' Not only the pregnancy of the mountain goats is known to us, but even stranger life cycles. We can penetrate the lair of the shyest of the animals. Sounds made by creatures of air and sea outside the range of the human ear can be heard by us. The long stretches of evolution are within our grasp.

'Can you lift out the whale with a gaff?' So effectively can we do this that whales are endangered species. And if Leviathan and Behemoth were mythological beasts then we have our techniques of demythologizing to tame them.

We know all mysteries and all knowledge – or almost all – and to remove mountains we do not need faith any more but only our earth-moving equipment.

With this knowledge the wonder has gone.

> Do not all charms fly
> At the mere touch of cold philosophy?
> There was an awful rainbow once in heaven:
> We know her woof, her texture; she is given
> In the dull catalogue of common things.
> Philosophy will clip an Angel's wings,
> Conquer all mysteries by rule and line,
> Empty the haunted air and gnomed mine –
> Unweave a rainbow.[2]

Keats felt that the discoveries of Newton had 'destroyed all the poetry of the rainbow by reducing it to the prismatic colours'. Ruskin admitted, 'I much question whether any one who knows optics, however religious he may be, can feel in equal degree the pleasure or reverence which an unlettered peasant may feel at the sight of a rainbow.'[3]

Yet the heart of religion is still trembling awe before the fascinating and fearful mystery.

Escapism is no answer. We cannot go back to the world of Job. The attempts of the Rechabites of the Old Testament or the modern Amish in America equally fail to preserve religion pure and undefiled.

---

[2] John Keats, *Lamia*, Part II, lines 229–237.
[3] Quoted in George P. Landow, *Images of Crisis*, Routledge & Kegan Paul 1982, pp. 166–167.

Knowledge cannot be destroyed, and even if in the first part of this commentary we tried to bracket it out, who can doubt but we failed.

Yet in a strange way increasing knowledge instead of destroying more and more of the mystery has restored it. The physicists are the great mystics of today. Michael Collins did not find God on the moon, though his experience in space changed him. No longer can he think of sunrise and sunset. He saw the earth a fragile globe, and the problems of ecology were transfigured for him. Other astronauts did discover God in the new mystery. The path to this mystery now is not through the unknown but through the known, through what is revealed by painstaking human search, not the sudden revelation from the heavens, not through ignorance but by way of breath-taking knowledge. Then we too see the Lord high and lifted up, with the whole universe as his glory, and we too fall on our faces before the likeness of the appearance of the glory of God.

One suggestion which goes back to the medieval Jewish philosopher Maimonides is that the Hebrew should be translated, '[I] repent of dust and ashes'. Job repudiates his laments, abandons his role as isolated sufferer lamenting among the ashes, and pushes remorse aside. He makes no confession of pride or guilt. His integrity is intact. He returns to normal life, for the appearance of God has vindicated his innocence and shown him that the way of approach to God is not by pursuing his claims based on the rule of reward and retribution. For he had been speaking in a way that made God a prisoner of retribution. It is not that justice does not reign in the world. Job has learnt that justice alone does not have the final say. 'The world of retribution – and not of temporal retribution only – is not where God dwells; at most God visits it. . . . Nothing, no human work however valuable, merits grace, for it if did grace would cease to be grace.'[4]

[4] So Gustavo Gutiérrez, *On Job*, pp. 86–89.

Other interpretations of Job's submission are:

1. Job totally capitulates to God, surrendering himself to his will and repenting of his arrogance in questioning God's justice.

2. Job arrives at a reconciliation with God. He has obtained a new understanding of God's rule of the world, and humbly acknowledges that God controls the universe.

3. Job's final confession is made tongue in cheek. He confesses a guilt he does not admit to appease the all-powerful deity. The fact that God accepts this confession shows his duplicity. The integrity of Job is shattered by God's lack of integrity. The poet is ironic to the last.

4. The closing speech is an act of defiance. Though he accepts the limitation of his knowledge of the working of the universe, he still sees God as the cruel tyrant he had pictured throughout the dialogue.

We are still troubled by that submission of Job. Silence, yes. The first submission is a valid response to the mystery. And the first part of the second accords with our understanding of the marvel of a God who lets himself be known. But why the repenting in or of dust and ashes? Even when we strip off the moral overtones of the word we are still unhappy with the thought that Job regrets his questions and his doubts. For ours is the age of the religious quest. The finding matters less to us. We would repudiate any suggestion that the quest is somehow wrong.

Perhaps the wisdom poem in ch. 28 has greater importance for an understanding of our poet's purpose than is generally recognized. Far from being an independent poem, complete in itself, which has somehow found its way into the dialogue at this point, it directs our attention to a key distinction between the two meanings of wisdom. Knowledge of the workings of the cosmos are hidden from human-kind. Only God knows this – and his questions to Job point this up. Even though our knowledge is greater than Job's and it is through the mystery of knowledge that we are reduced to humble awe, there must for ever be a religious agnosticism if God is truly to be God. But there *is* a wisdom accessible to mortals, a simple wisdom of reverence and goodness. Job had fulfilled the second, and our poet never tires of stressing this. Where he had failed was with the first. Now that he has seen God he has learnt the other part of true religion.

One insight still remains to be described. God set before Job all the wonders of the created world and proved to him his ignorance. But the world he displayed was a world which he had created. And while God did not mention the laws which govern the moral order, his words implied that he accepted responsibility for the whole of his creation – nature and evil alike. It was his world and he had made it like that. The laws controlling that world of morality, Job realized, are as mysterious as the incomprehensible ways of nature, and he gave up trying to puzzle them out. He no longer charged God with injustice because he did not invariably reward the good man with a comfortable prosperity and he did not always mete out to the evil man his just deserts. He was content to leave everything in God's hands, not because he now had proof of God's goodness, not because he had given up the unequal struggle with the all-powerful God, but because God had admitted that if there were any injustice, he was to blame, for he had made the world as it is.

The Christian must go further. We do not know whether this is the best of all possible worlds. We do not know whether God could have created beings who would always freely choose the good, though it seems to many that this proposal is incoherent. We do not know for certain whether this world is a vale of soul-making, though when we gaze around us we are uncertain whether this is a satisfactory answer to the problem of evil. But we have Christ, and the faith in a God who did not create this world, where good and evil are so strangely intermingled and where the best and kindest of men and women often suffer the most, and then leave it to its fate, or, like Hardy's President of the Immortals, take his sport with his creatures. He came into it himself, taking responsibility for what he had made and what men and women had made of his creation.

9 The end of the story

We come finally to the fairy-tale ending of the book, 'that dreadful ending' as one scholar described it. Does it not undermine the whole work? When we tried to place ourselves in the world of our poet we suggested that without the hope of a life after death Job had to be vindicated in this world, that the testing of Job's integrity was over, and that such a rounding off was essential to the plot. The twentieth-century Christian is not satisfied.

The problem is not that the Christian wishes to take into account the possibility of a future life, though that is important for many who wish to construct their theodicies. Life in this present world may be the only way in which spiritual beings could come to a free relationship with God that is founded on faith and is not forced upon them by the overpowering glory of God or the distortion of trust by the connection between goodness and reward. To make sense of this, however, demands that the present existence opens into a larger life beyond the grave.[1] The difficulty concerns the fact that there is no restoration for many good man and women who suffer as Job did, and we find it difficult to see the value of suffering which crushes the spirit and has no outcome but destruction.

The 'vale of soul-making' answer to the problem of suffering has one fatal defect – so many souls are not 'made'. Suffering can enoble the character. Suffering can bring out hidden strengths and lead to the patience of which Job has become the proverbial symbol. One of

[1] For the best discussion of this see John Hick, *Evil and the God of Love*, Macmillan 1966, ²1977. Related to this is the question of life after death, and John Hick has discussed this in *Death and Eternal Life*, Collins 1976, Harper and Row 1977.

my most vivid memories is of the husband of a church worker who had no time for parsons and was never seen inside our little village chapel where his wife loved to be, cleaning, decorating, setting out the harvest festival gifts, preparing for communion. Then his wife had a debilitating stroke, and he tended her with loving care until she died, and took up the work she had done within the church.

But suffering can equally make the victim bitter, destroy the beauty of body and spirit, reduce a man or a woman to something less than human. With the sweet memory of that husband I recall the warped body of his wife and her weakness and tears.

J. B. Phillips tells how his mother became increasingly ill. 'She rarely complained and then only of tiredness, but I now know that she suffered from cancer in various parts of her body for some ten years. She finally died in hospital in 1921 (when my father could no longer nurse her). I used to sit with her sometimes in the summer of that year, and she had become a terrible sight. She had lost almost all her hair, her body had shrunken to a tortured lump of flesh, and the pain was very great. Most of the time in those last months she hardly knew us, and I grew angrier and angrier that God could allow such a terrifying physical and mental degradation to happen to such a wonderful woman. I gave up my religious faith utterly, for what use was prayer and talk of the love of God when I returned daily to this horrible caricature of the spritely, witty mother I had known and loved?'[2] To point to the self-sacrifice and loving care that are brought out in those who look after the stricken loved ones is no answer. And often the strain of caring brings mental breakdown to those whose every hour is tied to the needs of the relative who is aged or ill. J. B. Phillips found faith again, as did Mary Craig, but many have not.

I do not believe our poet set out to construct an answer to the problem of suffering, for if he did he certainly failed most miserably. Yet even with his different purpose of revealing the nature of true religion, his final narrative seems to undercut all the insights he has brought before us in his poetry. For this is no longer our world. Worse, are we to suppose that the seven new sons and three beautiful daughters simply 'replaced' those who had died? Did Job never give a thought to his first family? It is easy to understand why so many have thought that the conclusion was added by a lesser writer.

Some scholars have found a meaning in these closing verses. One supposes that the author's hands were tied by the folk-story. 'To have made the hero die in leprosy would have been too audacious a

<hr>

[2] J. B. Phillips, *The Price of Success*, Hodder & Stoughton 1984, p. 37.

contradiction of what may well have been a well-authenticated tradition.' Perhaps his acceptance of the tradition showed that it was not his intention to deny that prosperity often attended righteousness but only to prove that this was not invariable nor inevitable.[3]

Another suggests that there are three 'supplementary messages': (1) There had to be a public vindication of Job and God's commendation in 42.7 clears his reputation and affirms that he was innocent of the charges laid against him by the friends; (2) the author wished to declare that the orthodox teaching of the friends was inadequate; not that God disapproved of everything that they said, but he had to tell them that 'they were not defenders of the faith but stumbling-blocks to the faithful'; God has 'a healthy mistrust for his more self-assured supporters'; and (3) the author wanted to show that the traditional connection between goodness and prosperity is not totally false – hence the restoration of Job's fortunes.[4]

Yet others see the restoration as a sign of divine generosity, emphasized by the doubling of Job's possessions,[5] or as an indication that God is not a capricious tyrant but, while he may withdraw his favour for a season, his love is for a life-time.

But what of those who live lives of agony and die without ever seeing the evidence of God's grace? Ours is a harsher world than the ending of Job admits. For myself I find I can understand why our poet felt compelled to end his book as he did. I cannot see what message it can have for us today.

---

[3] James Strahan, *The Book of Job Interpreted*, p. 350.

[4] J. C. L. Gibson, *Job*, pp. 264–66.

[5] Cf. F. I. Anderson: 'It would be absurd to say that He must keep Job in miserable poverty in order to safeguard the theology. These gifts at the end are gestures of grace, not rewards for virtue' (*Job*, IVP 1976, p. 294).

APPENDIX 1

Ancient Parallels to Job

Suffering is universal, and it is no surprise that writings which deal with suffering are found in many literatures. Parallels to Job are closest in the Old Testament. Psalms of complaint contain many lines that are similar to ideas in Job, and the psalmists express perplexity at the prosperity of the wicked and the suffering of the innocent.[1] The great nature psalms also reflect the wonder of the divine speeches and Elihu's descriptions of the natural world.[2] Job's curse on the day of his birth has an obvious parallel in Jer. 20.14–18, while scholars have drawn attention to further phrases in Proverbs,[3] Lamentations,[4] Isaiah,[5] and other books which have close similarities to lines in Job. Job 7.17–18 seems to be a parody of Ps. 8, while the themes of the righteous sufferer and the transcendence of God are also found in Isa. 40–55. Despite the non-Israelite setting, the book is closer to the rest of the Old Testament than to external literature from the ancient Middle East.

Nevertheless, comparisons have often been drawn between Job and three Mesopotamian texts, and while we do not know whether our poet copied from these or even knew them, they help us to put away our modern dress and clothe ourselves in the culture of the world of Job.

The first differs from Job in that it is not a dialogue. The writing usually referred to by the first line, 'I will praise the Lord of Wisdom', is the plaint of a Babylonian in a high position who has been struck down by an illness that he describes in great detail. The poem, as its title shows, is a thanksgiving hymn for deliverance, and the problem

[1] Cf. Pss. 6; 10; 13; 22; 38; 39; 49; 73; 88.
[2] Cf. particularly the great nature psalm 104.
[3] Job and the friends quote or refer to proverbial sayings. The following may be noted: Prov. 3.11 // Job 5.17; Prov. 3.14–15; 8.11, 19 // Job 28.15–19; Prov. 8.25b // Job 15.7b; Prov. 13.9 // Job 18.5–6; Prov. 15.11 // Job 26.6; Prov. 22.8 // Job 4.8.
[4] Cf. Lam. 3.7–15 // Job 6.4; 9.18b; 12.4; 19.8; 30.9.
[5] Cf. Isa. 41.20a // Job 12.9b; Isa. 44.24c // Job 9.8a; Isa. 51.15a // Job 26.12a; Isa. 53.9b // Job 16.17a; Isa. 59.4d // Job 15.35a.

of why the righteous should suffer is touched on only lightly. As in many of the psalms, the sufferer vividly describes the illness from which he has been delivered.

> Feebleness has seized my whole body,
> Concussion has fallen upon my flesh.
>
> Paralysis has grasped my arms,
> Impotence has fallen on my knees,
> My feet forget their motion. . . .
>
> When grain is served, I eat it like stinkweed,
> Beer, the life of mankind, is distasteful to me. . . .
>
> I spend the night in my dung like a ox,
> And wallow in my excrement like a sheep.[6]

The writer affirms his piety, however, and at one point hesitatingly charges the god (whom he refers to as 'he' in a similar way to Job in a number of places) with causing his sufferings, saying, 'His hand was heavy upon me', although Job is far more forthright in blaming God for his distress. He also complains that

> My god has not come to my rescue in taking me by the hand,
> Nor has my goddess shown pity on me by going at my side.[7]

Whether the writer expresses a hope of release that may be set alongside Job 19.25 is uncertain. There are apparently textual difficulties, and translations of the Akkadian vary. Lambert offers the reading:

> But I know the day for my whole family,
> when, among my friends, their Sun-god will have mercy.[8]

After he has received promises of restoration in dreams, Marduk begins to bring deliverance – and the tablet breaks off. The sufferer is restored, therefore, as is Job at the end of the book.

A noteworthy feature in the Babylonian poem is the assertion that humans cannot know what is pleasing to the gods.

> I wish I knew that these things were pleasing to one's god!
> What is proper to oneself is an offence to one's god.
> What in one's own heart seems despicable is proper to one's god.

---

[6] W. G. Lambert, *Babylonian Wisdom Literature*, Clarendon Press 1960, pp. 43–45.
[7] Ibid., p. 46.
[8] Ibid.

Who knows the will of the gods in heaven?
Who understands the plans of the underworld gods?
Where have mortals learnt the way of a god?[9]

Job, by contrast, never doubts that what the human conscience regards as right is also right with God. Indeed, it might even be claimed that Job's willingness to accuse God of acting unjustly reveals that he is recognizing a justice to which even God should submit.

While 'I will praise the Lord of wisdom' differs from Job in being a monologue, there are dialogues in both Mesopotamia and Egypt. The famous 'Babylonian Theodicy' is an elaborate acrostic of twenty-seven stanzas of eleven lines each (cf. Ps. 119 for the form). In this a sufferer appeals to his friend to listen to his tale of anguish. He was left an orphan, and has been oppressed by the powerful while receiving no protection from the gods. The friend shows more sympathy than the friends of Job. Only towards the end does he say:

O wise one, O savant, who masters knowledge,
In your anguish you blaspheme the god.
The divine mind, like the centre of the heavens, is remote;
Knowledge of it is difficult; the masses do not know it.[10]

In general he simply affirms that the reward of piety is prosperity, and insists that the wicked are punished. This the sufferer denies:

Those who neglect the god go the way of prosperity,
While those who pray to the goddess are impoverished and
    dispossessed.[11]

He claims that he sought the will of his god from his youth, but his god decreed destitution instead of wealth. Like Job he complains,

The dregs of humanity, like the rich and opulent, treat me with
    contempt.[12]

It is the wicked who are praised and supported:

People extol the word of a strong man who is trained in murder,
But bring down the powerless who has done no wrong.
They confirm the wicked whose crime is [. . .],
Yet suppress the honest man who heeds the will of his god.[13]

[9] Lambert, *op. cit.*, p. 41.
[10] Ibid., p. 87.
[11] Ibid., p. 75.
[12] Ibid., p. 87.
[13] Ibid.

Solemnly they speak in favour of a rich man,
'He is a king', they say, 'riches go at his side.'
But they harm a poor man like a thief,
They lavish slander upon him and plot his murder,
Making him suffer every evil like a criminal, because he has no
    protection.
Terrifyingly they bring him to his end, and extinguish him like a
                                                    flame.[14]

The poem ends suddenly, and we are not told what the fate of the sufferer is.

The parallels to Job are clear, but in Job there is a far greater sense of the problem of evil and a deeper understanding of the involvement of God in the affairs of human beings.

A more ancient prayer by a pious sufferer comes from about 2000 BC. In this text, which has been called the 'Sumerian Job', an anonymous man has been afflicted by misfortune for no apparent reason. He does not protest but asks for deliverance, admitting that no one is free from guilt.

They, the great wise ones, proclaim a true and just word:
'A sinless child was never born of its mother,
there has never been an innocent boy from ancient times.'[15]

In the end, rather in the manner of Job in the prose narrative, he is heard and saved, and he praises his god.

The bitter tears and lamentations of the man found a hearing with
    his god,
when the cries of woe and weeping with which he was over-
    whelmed had soothed the heart of his god for him.
The just utterance, the simple, pure word which he spoke was
    accepted by his god . . .
He changed the man's grief into joy . . .
The man did not cease to praise his god.[16]

We are closer here to the laments of the Psalms than to Job, and there is little striving to understand why a righteous man should suffer. Nor, it will be noticed, is this a dialogue.

---

[14] Ibid., p. 89.
[15] Walter Beyerlin, ed., *Near Eastern Religious Texts relating to the Old Testament*, SCM Press and Westminster Press 1978, p. 141. Cf. Eliphaz's assertion in Job 15.14–16, and Bildad's in 25.4–6.
[16] Ibid., p. 142.

Even earlier than these wisdom type writings a personal name 'What-is-my-guilt?' has been found, surely implying that there was a sense of undeserved suffering. A line from a dialogue between a man and his god reads, 'The crime which I did I know not', which has been variously taken to be an asssertion of innocence and an admission of sin, and in another text a sufferer says, 'I have been treated as one who has committed a sin against his god', with the implication that he does not accept that he is guilty of sin. The link between sin and suffering was recognized in Mesopotamia, and some individuals questioned whether they were justly punished.[17]

Dialogues are found in Egypt, but although there is often a note of pessimism and suicide is contemplated because there is no justice in the world, the anxiety aroused by a sense of punishment for unknown personal sins is not found. Rather the writers complain that they are the victims of social wrongs.

One of the most moving is 'The Protests of the Eloquent Peasant', coming from about 2000 BC. Like Job it has a story framework. A peasant is robbed by the vassal of the chief steward and refuses to abandon his claim for justice, even though it costs him beatings and threats to his life. In the end he receives the property of the man who seized his goods. Some passages recall Job's assertions of his virtue. In his appeal to the steward the peasant says: 'Thou art the father of the orphan, the husband of the widow, the brother of the divorcee, and the apron of him that is motherless'.[18] He argues that justice should be done for the sake of the god, the Lord of justice.

Even closer to Job is the 'Dispute over Suicide', dated at about the same time. A man who is oppressed by the injustice in the world longs for death and his soul tries to dissuade him. Like Job it has a prose introduction and conclusion, within which is set a poetic dialogue. Social injustice underlies the man's desire for death:

> (One's) fellows are evil;
> the friends of today do not love.
>
> Hearts are rapacious:
> Every man seizes his fellow's goods.
>
> The gentle man has perished,
> (But) the violent man has access to everybody.

[17] W. G. Lambert, op. cit., pp. 10–11.
[18] Translation by John A. Wilson in *Ancient Near Eastern Texts*, ed. James B. Pritchard, Princeton University Press 1950, p. 408. Cf. Job 29.12–17; 31.16–21, 32.

(Even) the calm of face is wicked;
Goodness is rejected everywhere.

There are no righteous;
The land is left to those who do wrong.

The sin which treads the earth,
It has no end.[19]

The hope of a future life in which the dead become living gods is a promise that Job cannot accept, however, and although there are similarities in the relief which death may bring, Sheol is very different from the Egyptian's expectation.

Death is in my sight today
(Like) the recovery of a sick man,
Like going out into the open after a confinement.

Death is in my sight today
Like the odor of myrrh
Like sitting under an awning on a breezy day.

Death is in my sight today
Like the passing away of rain,
Like the return of men to their houses from an expedition.

Death is in my sight today
Like the longing of a man to see his house (again)
After he has spent many years held in captivity.[20]

Job fits into the literature and thought of the ancient Middle East. Both the ideas and the form can be paralleled. None of the writings so far discovered, however, can match its intensity and religious depth.

[19] Ibid., p. 406.
[20] Ibid., p. 407. Cf. Job 3.17–19.

APPENDIX 2

Alternative Interpretations of Job

In this commentary we have taken the REB text as a valid translation of the Hebrew and have attempted to understand the book in its final form. The answers that are given to questions of whether any passages come from a later hand than that of the original poet and what the history of the development of the book may have been have a marked influence on the interpretation of its meaning. Here it is only possible to outline five of the ways in which the book has been read.

N. H. Snaith[1] argued that the whole book comes from the same writer, but that it was written in three stages.

The poet's first intention was to tell a story similar to the Babylonian 'I will praise the Lord of wisdom'. It would have been an orthodox piece of wisdom literature with no particular theological theory. He rewrote the folk-story, inserted Job's soliloquies and the Yahweh speeches, with the two-stage submission by Job.

But the poet continued to ponder his hero, in much that same way that Goethe was held captive by the Faust legend throughout his life. He now began to question the conventional orthodoxy and added chs. 4–28, adapting the prose framework to include the three friends. Job is still orthodox, believing that there is an answer to the problem of evil and that if he could only find his way into God's presence all would be well, although he challenges the friends' account of retribution because he affirms his own innocence.

Finally the author added the Elihu speeches by the angry young man who attacks the old orthodoxy. Elihu is not primarily concerned with the problem of suffering but asserts that the gulf between human beings and the transcendent God remains. He has no solution, although the idea of intermediary is mooted (Job 33.23–28), and concludes that God is all-powerful and we must submit to him.

[1] *The Book of Job: Its Origin and Purpose*, SCM Press and A. R. Allenson 1968.

W. A. Irwin[2] has written a remarkably perceptive short commentary. He believes he can trace the book's long and intricate history. We need not follow his critical reconstruction, except for noting that Irwin believes that the original poetic work consisted solely of the dialogue in Job 3–27, and even this ended in tattered fragments. This means that he finds a different message in each stage of the development of the book.

The prologue affirms that disinterested piety is a reality, and asserts that suffering comes from the Satan, not from God.

The epilogue (distinct from the prologue!) recognizes that Job is the hero of the dialogue, but the writer seems to be able to say only that if a sufferer has the toughness to endure, all will come out right in the end.

The Elihu speeches (and Irwin thinks that the four speeches are independent and have slightly different emphases) teach that suffering comes as a warning, to recall the sufferer to right living.

The Yahweh speeches, for all their genius, speak of nothing but the might and omniscience of God. Showing no concern with morality, they contribute nothing to the problem of innocent suffering.

The central dialogue describes a spiritual pilgrimage from uncritical orthodoxy to a faith and hope grounded in experience. Within this the high moments are recognition by Job that, despite the great evils in life, there are great moments of joy (10.12–13), the indispensable role of the intermediary, who is an intercessor with God, even though he is not clearly delineated, and Job's daring hope that after he has passed through death he will meet God.

The more recent commentators accept that the poet planned the work as an artistic whole, and adopt an approach that is strongly influenced by English literary criticism. Thus J. G. Janzen holds that the 'church can properly hear its Bible as Scripture only when it reads it as literature'.[3] In particular he finds a wide use of irony in the book, and the use of four different kinds of question, real questions seeking information, rhetorical questions, impossible questions pointing to human frailty and the limits of human understanding, and existential questions which are not meant to be answered but pose a goal toward which one has to 'live'. The central issue is whether the book *can* be read as a whole. He believes that it is impossible to strip away the

[2] 'Job' in M. Black and H. H. Rowley, eds., *Peake's Commentary on the Bible*, Nelson 1962, pp. 391–408.
[3] *Job*, p. 15, quoting D. J. A. Clines.

prose framework and read the dialogues by themselves. Chapter 28 is a meditation by Job after his argument with the friends has ended and before he presents the survey of his life in chs. 29–31, in which he sums up the human search for wisdom and concludes that primal wisdom is withheld from human beings and its functional equivalent is piety and uprightness. Elihu is introduced to provide a further critique of traditional religious attitudes. The third cycle of speeches seems to be in disarray, but it is possible to see them as a deliberate 'tangle of incoherent voices', with Job quoting the friends wholesale to indicate that he will no longer listen to them because he knows what they will say already.

In a similar way N. C. Habel[4] treats the book as a literary whole, though admitting that the third cycle of speeches has suffered dislocation. He thinks that the book is modelled on 'traditional biblical narrative' in which speeches carry the plot forward. The outline of the plot is signalled by the introductions of Job (1.1–5), the friends (2.11–13), and Elihu (32.1–5), which divide it into three 'movements', each containing 'episodes'. The Sumerian and Babylonian 'Job' texts have the same skeletal plot structure, which the author of Job has adapted and extended. The central theme is the conflict between 'the integrity of the Creator and the integrity of a particular mortal'. Job's moral goodness is fair game for testing. Yet the way God agrees to test it throws the justice of his rule into question. It is this which is relentlessly probed in the dialogue. Elihu is the arbiter, foreshadowed in 31.35 in Job's summons. Since no arbiter came, Elihu assumes the role. The divine speeches depict a world controlled by the freedom of God within the constraints of his cosmic design, but a mechanical system of reward and punishment is not a necessary part of that order. Hence Job withdraws his legal suit, for there is no point in pursuing it when retributive justice is not to be found in the cosmic scene, and he confesses that he did not understand that design.

Gutiérrez[5] holds that the central question of the book is 'How are we to talk about God?' and he approaches this question from the situation of the suffering of the innocent in Latin America. In the first part of his study he examines the prose sections of Job together with Job's speech in ch. 3. The book is built upon the wager, Can human beings have a disinterested faith in God? Are they capable of continuing to

---

[4] *The Book of Job.*
[5] *On Job: God-talk and the Suffering of the Innocent.*

assert their faith without expecting anything in return? The author of the book believes it is possible, and Job is his spokesman.

In the other two sections Gutiérrez develops the view that the book combines the languages of prophecy and contemplation, the first in the main dialogue and the Elihu speeches, the second chiefly in the words of Yahweh and Job's responses. Job discovers in the end that 'the language the prophets use in speaking of God must be supplemented by the language of contemplation and worship.'

The problem of divine justice does underlie the argument, as does the problem of suffering. But the poet's purpose is to show that if we reduce our thinking to the justice of God this reduces God to an idol. Unless we are prepared to allow God to be the final mystery, free to express the 'gratuitousness' of his love, a love which is utterly unbounded and unmerited and reaches out to the whole of creation, we distort the nature of justice and the demand for just dealings which is laid upon us.

The key to the book is Job's second reply to God. Job does not repent of what he has already said; he repudiates his lamentation and dejection. He realises that he had been speaking of God in a way that implied that God was a prisoner of a particular way of understanding justice, and he now rejects this total outlook. Justice alone does not have the final say. Grace is what gives full meaning to justice.

APPENDIX 3

The Problem of Evil

Teachers will wish to go beyond the book of Job to the questions about evil which the book raises, and while preachers will beware of turning their sermons into lectures, they will often find that preaching on Job leads to discussions about the problem of suffering. There is no space to deal in any detail with these issues. Indeed it is not my intention to offer a philosophical debate. Rather, starting from the book of Job, I shall set out a few observations which may encourage readers to consider the problem further.[1]

The dialogue in the book of Job ended with Job's abasement before the mysterious creator. No answer to the problem of suffering was given, and some would say that the writer did not attempt any. We might suppose that his answer was that no human can puzzle out why suffering exists in a world which a good God has created.

We saw, however, that God accepted responsibility for the world as it is. He is the creator. This at least rules out several options. Our poet accepts that God exists. We cannot escape the problem by a retreat into atheism (though as we have already pointed out, many people have become atheists *because of* the suffering which they find in the world). Secondly, the poet rejects the view that there are two rival spiritual beings, one evil and one good. The Satan is not the Devil: he is one of God's servants in his heavenly court. Thirdly, Job's suffering is real: the suggestion that evil is an illusion is not permitted as a way out. Finally, the poet shows no knowledge of a Fall.[2] We

---

[1] Besides the major discussion by John Hick already noted, Peter Vardy has a useful chapter in *God of Our Fathers?*, Darton, Longman & Todd 1987, as has Ninian Smart in *Philosophers and Religious Truth*, SCM Press and Ryerson Press 1964. Other studies are: A. Plantinga, *God, Freedom and Evil*, Harper & Row 1974, Allen & Unwin 1975, and P. Geach, *Providence and Evil*, CUP 1971.

[2] This is the traditional Christian explanation of sin and suffering, yet it is now impossible for the thoughtful believer on historical and theological grounds. Knowledge of the development of the expanding universe and the evolution of life on earth, and a recognition of the genre of the stories in Genesis make it inconceivable that there ever was an age of primal innocence from which the

cannot say that suffering is the consequence of human sin, even if it is not the sufferer himself who has committed the particular sin for which the punishment is being visited upon him. Any suggestion that the suffering is retribution is explicitly rejected.

The problem can now be defined like this. God is said to be omnipotent and perfectly good. Yet evil exists in the world which he has created. This suggests either that he is not all-powerful or that his intentions are less than benign. (Or that there is no God – but this was never contemplated in the Old Testament and we shall pass it by here, since we are not intending to argue for the existence of God.)

It is important to be clear about what we mean by omnipotent and perfectly good.

While some would defend the position that God can do anything whatever and that even the logic of reasoning might have been created differently, most people would accept that God cannot do things which are logically absurd, such as making a stone which was too big for him to lift. This would imply that he has created a universe in which the patterns of interaction which we have grown accustomed to call 'laws of nature' apply, though our understanding of what these laws are has changed with fresh discoveries.

The exact meaning of God's goodness is more difficult. We saw that the Babylonian poem 'I will praise the Lord of wisdom' contains the assertion that humans cannot know what is pleasing to the gods. In other words, the gods may have a different idea of goodness from men and women. The Old Testament, however, apart from Qoheleth, is quite certain that human and divine justice are the same. Indeed Abraham can even ask God, 'Shall not the judge of all the earth do what is just?' (Gen. 18.25), perhaps pointing to a 'natural law' to which even God must be subject. Certainly Job has no doubt that what is just to humans is the standard by which God's justice is to be assessed. Many philosophers would doubt whether the matter is quite as simple and would wish to say that God's goodness is only analogous to ours, and that his idea of what is good, because of his

---

original humans fell. Sin is indeed universal – here is the truth of the doctrine of 'original sin' – but this is not an entail from a first disobedience. To suggest that the suffering which we find in animal and human existence is due to that disobedience is immoral and incredible. How can we suppose it is just that a baby should die of cancer because a supposed ancestor ate the fruit of a tree which the creator had forbidden him to touch? How can we imagine that such a trivial action should somehow 'infect' the whole of the universe and lead to the massive and unintelligible suffering which we see? As for the supposition of fallen angels, this owes more to intertestamental sectarian writings (and to Milton) than to the Jewish and Christian scriptures.

greater knowledge, may differ from ours. Nevertheless they would feel bound to affirm that actions which would be outrageously evil if we did them must also be evil if done by God. Job at least believed so.

We also need to examine more closely the assertion that evil exists in the world.

The disasters which befell Job are of two kinds. The oxen and donkeys were carried off by a raiding band of Sabaeans, and the Chaldeans seized the camels, in both cases killing those tending them. The sheep, on the other hand were burned up by 'God's fire' which 'flashed from heaven'. The reference is presumably to the lightning. The eldest brother's house was brought down upon the heads of Job's sons and daughters by a 'whirlwind' that 'swept across the desert', and no rationalization is needed here. Job is said to have been stricken by 'running sores' by 'the Adversary', but again we tend to see this as a 'natural' illness, even though we are unable to determine clinically what its exact nature was, and in any case the descriptions within the dialogue seem to imply a rather more extensive illness than a skin disease. Thus we would distinguish between natural disasters and evil caused by human beings, between natural and moral evils.

Suffering caused by our fellow human beings is often, and probably correctly, explained by the 'free-will defence': that in order to make it possible for men and women freely to choose good rather than evil and to enter willingly into fellowship with God it had to be possible for them to do evil. This is not the whole answer, however, and we need to remember that Job was unwilling to let God off the final responsibility, and we suggested that one meaning to be extracted from the divine speeches was that God himself accepted responsibility for the world which he had created. It becomes necessary to accept that this is the only kind of world, or the best kind, to achieve God's purposes. Those purposes are commonly seen as providing an environment in which men and women would have the opportunity to develop their moral sensibilities and freely choose good rather than evil. It is also a world in which God is sufficiently hidden to make fellowship with him a matter of faith and not to compel allegiance through the power of his immediate presence. The question is, did there have to be the possibility of so many and such monstrous evils, and does the possible good which resulted from God's decision outweigh the vast amount of innocent suffering which exists in the world?

The book of Job accords with our modern sensitivities in that it is the 'natural' disasters against which Job inveighs most strongly, whether it is his own sickness or the 'punishments' which he claims innocent people often suffer.

It is usual to attempt to lessen the impact of these disasters. Some pain is a warning to the body against greater dangers. Yet even this only slightly reduces the pressure of the problem. The pain of appendicitis was useless before surgery was available. Many pains, especially those which afflict women, seem purposeless. And some of the most serious diseases produce no pain in the early stages when a cure would have been possible.

Further, if we are to have a physical world, human bodies are going to be crushed when two cars meet on the same bit of road. We could neither envisage a world in which the regularities to which we give the shorthand name of 'natural laws' could not be relied upon, nor could we cope with a situation where water suddenly went uphill or gravity stopped, even for the smallest part of a second. In such a world life would be impossible and science could not even begin to interpret its functioning.

To many this is an adequate answer, even though it also means that the cancer and the deformed baby are also part of the inevitabilities of an ordered physical universe. The lightning and the whirlwind in our poet's story have to be accepted as having no moral significance. Others would argue that the cost of creating a world such as ours is too great. God is responsible and since he is omniscient as well as omnipotent he must have foreseen what would happen. He cannot be regarded as perfectly good. This might be met by suggesting, as the conclusion of the dialogue implies, that human beings do not know the whole working of the universe or the design of God. Mystery remains.

So far we have pictured God in a rather deistic way, as the creator who set the universe off on its course and then allowed it to evolve and men and women to exercise their freedom to the full. Many today would be inclined to adopt such a position, and it is striking that Christian scientists have tended to be better at presenting a theistic view of the creation and evolution of the universe and life on our planet than they have at constructing a convincing concept of providence.[3] This is not the place to enter into questions of 'miracle'

---

[3] On the relation between science and religion there is now an extensive literature. The most accessible books are: A. Ford, *Universe: God, Man and Science*, Hodder & Stoughton 1986; J. Polkinghorne, *One World*, SPCK 1986, *Science and Creation: The Search for Understanding*, SPCK 1988, *Science and Providence*, SPCK 1989; R. Stannard, *Science and the Renewal of Belief*, SCM Press 1982. More difficult and extensive is A. R. Peacocke, *Creation and the World of Science*, OUP 1979.

and divine intervention, and it must suffice to state baldly that the most serious argument against the working of special miracles by God is the moral objection, that if God does work wonders to help those who pray to him, why did he remain silent when the greatest human tragedies were taking place.

If in the end we are unwilling to remain with mystery, as the writer of Job left us, placing fellowship with God above intellectual understanding of the problem of suffering and satisfied with the religious encounter, then the 'vale of soul-making' explanation seems the best resort. Questions still press in, however. It would have been no answer for Job. He could only case a wistful glance at the life after death and return to a world in which the only expectation was of the gloom of Sheol when his earthly course was run. The Christian has a greater confidence, though doubts must surely persist for very many. From a moral aspect it has to be asked whether the extent and severity of the suffering can ever be regarded as the necessary cost for the making of souls, especially when many souls seem to be crushed under their sorrows rather than lifted to heroic virtue. Only a cross and a wounded God remain for us to cling to.

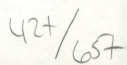